Life

It Is What It Is

A book by

Lisa Sugarman

ISBN: 1494798131
ISBN 13: 9781494798130
Library of Congress Control Number: 2013923588
CreateSpace Independent Publishing Platform
North Charleston, South Carolina

Dedication

This book is dedicated, with every ounce of my love and thanks, to my family and friends who inspired everything on these pages and have always brought out the very best in me. It's for everyone who believed I could even when I didn't.

But most of all, this book is for my girlies, Lulu and Rye, who've put up with my crazy all these years and loved me in spite of it. And for you, Mom—rock of all rocks and the mother of all mothers. You gave me the gift of a beautiful life and showed me, by example, how to squeeze the absolute most out of it. This book is proof. And for Ma and Dad—in-laws who make the word "in-laws" seem silly because you've always been like the real McCoy. And the rest of the Sugarpeople, who supported my dreams like they were your own. I couldn't have done it without you. I'm one lucky broad.

And last, but never least, for my husband, Dave, the greatest guy there ever was. You've had my back and kept me sane and loved me more than anyone's ever been loved. I do you the most, babe. This one's for you, Virgil. We did it!

Table of Contents

Preface

Holy crap, you actually bought it! I can't believe it. And you opened it! This is amazing! I'm totally humbled. Of all the choices you had out there for something to inspire you, you chose my book. And that's just mind blowing to me. So thank you. Really.

Now I'm not exactly sure why you're here, nor does it really matter. I'm honestly just thrilled that you are. Maybe you think I have all the answers for how to live the perfect life. (God, please don't think I have all the answers. Please.) I don't want you to get the wrong idea. Because I don't.

What I *do* have are little nuggets of truth straight from the mind of someone whose life is probably just as crazy as yours—someone who's learned that the real secret to living a beautiful, mostly happy life is nothing more than attitude. It's really that simple. Because no one can live a totally idyllic life. That's just ridiculous.

Look, I'm a fierce believer that the cup is always half full. I have to be. Life doesn't make sense to me any other way. And that's the thread you'll see woven into everything I write. My bottom line is that *we can't control what life throws at us; we can only control how we receive it.*

Life is beautiful, but life is also ugly and imperfect, and people need someone to remind them that it's *supposed* to be that way. The average person needs someone they can connect with—a regular, average, positive person—to reassure them that with the right attitude and guidance, anyone can be happy and fulfilled most of the time.

Ironically, there is no such thing as perfection, and deep down I think we all know it. There's no formula to make it all work because life isn't static, it's fluid, and it expects *us* to adapt. So what I suggest here in this book is that we embrace the reality that we're *supposed* to be imperfect, we're *supposed* to screw up, and we're *supposed* to make bad decisions and lose our way. I guess you could say it's like tough love for the soul.

We're all so scattered and overwhelmed most of the time that what I think people really need are little, easy-to-digest chunks of reality they can relate to that make sense to them in their daily lives. Ideas that inspire them. Stories that reassure them that they're not alone—that we're all dealing with the same craziness every day.

Most people who follow my column say they read it because it sounds like I'm having a conversation with them from a bathroom stall. And that's why they like it. And hopefully you will, too.

One brief, but necessary, point of clarity though, before you dive in. I think it's important that I introduce the book's main character before you start reading. Otherwise you might be a little confused, since she appears in just about all of my columns.

The main character is a little unorthodox. Actually, it's not even a real character. It's an entire town. My town. Marblehead, Massachusetts. I know, it's a little wacky to think of a whole town as a single character, but Marblehead is a pretty unique place. And if you lived here, you'd understand.

There are about twenty thousand of us all crammed onto one nineteen-square-mile peninsula. So while the rest of the world has six whole degrees of separation, Marblehead barely has one. Because in most cases, everyone knows just about everyone else. And since I grew up here, live here, coach here, and work in the school system here, I myself have little or no degrees. I know just about everyone. So I have a pretty unique perspective as a columnist. And because almost everything I write about either has to do with Marblehead or the people who live here, Marblehead as the main character was the obvious choice. Besides, she has too many human qualities not to be—she's beautiful and mysterious and welcoming and stony and warm and modest and vain and pretentious and humble and charming and aloof and noble and materialistic and enduring and lovable, all at the same time—she's a perfect cocktail of everything that makes a person tick. It's all part of her charm.

But keep one very important thing in mind while you're reading: whatever happens here, happens everywhere. And that's the beauty. Even though I'm writing about the people and the places I know the best, everything I write about is fully transferable to anyplace and anyone. It's all happening to you or to someone you know.

So there. Now you're informed. You've got the whole backstory so you're locked and loaded and ready to go. I hope you enjoy the trip.

How do I use the Book?

Since most of us barely have time to zip up our fly before we leave the house, it made sense to me to write a book that people could digest quickly, that would fill you up and give you the most bang for your buck, kind of like brown rice. Read it in the bathroom. Keep it by the bed or in the car or on your e-reader. Read one column at a time or read ten. Read them to your husband or your friends or your kids. Read it with your book club, a handful of columns at a time, out loud, with plenty of wine and bitching in between. Read them as a constant reminder that life, by nature, is chaotic and disjointed, even on the best of days. Read them to remind yourself that you *always* have the power to choose happiness. Or maybe read them just to remind yourself that life is not a straight line, and it's always a work in progress.

Run for Your Life

Printed October 2009

I run. I run a lot. Less than some, more than others. I'm not an ultra-marathoner or one of the elites. I'm no one glamorous, just a soccer mom, a semiregular columnist, and a reading tutor.

I run because I never could and now I can. It's simple, really. Growing up, I played school sports and ran my share of suicide drills on the middle school soccer field, but I could never run distances— just didn't have the endurance for it.

I used to envy people I saw running. I envied the solitude and the strength and the peace of it. So I trained for and ran my first 10K in my late twenties. I finished, but the only things behind me were the ambulance and some woman pushing sixty (I smoked her at the finish). It was brutal and exhilarating all at once. I loved everything about it.

Then I had my kids, and I stopped running. I stopped for almost a decade. I'm really not sure why; I just stopped. Then, on a family holiday in Florida five years ago (at thirty-six), I went out for a walk that morphed into a run. And I haven't stopped since. I can't say why I started to run that day; I just did. I just couldn't sit there watching people around me run anymore. We all have our tipping points, and I guess that was mine.

I've gotten faster over the years. Nothing dramatic, but definitely noticeable. I've run 5Ks, 10Ks, and half marathons, and now my husband and I are running our first marathon later this month.

But I don't run for speed (anyone who sees me running knows that); I run for clarity. I'd be lying if I said I don't run for the obvious reasons like good cardio, to keep weight off, to stay fit. But mostly I run for the mental health of it.

Funnily enough, the more I run, the clearer things are. And when you do any kind of distance running, you've got a *lot* of time to kill. There are Zunes and iPods, but those will only take you so far before they become monotonous and even a little annoying. So eventually you're going to wind up just running.

And it's amazing what your mind conjures up when you're alone in your own head for any real length of time. It's a real exercise in isolation. Even though life is moving all around you, you're completely alone. It's like you're in some whacked-out version of solitary confinement that moves.

But I actually do much more than just run when I run. I solve problems, make decisions, plan out my day, mediate fights—I pretty much run the gamut (no pun, I swear). I'm usually so engrossed in whatever I'm thinking about that it's like I'm somewhere else altogether. It's amazing I haven't fallen on my face yet. (OK, well, maybe I have, but it's only happened a couple of times and not when anyone was looking.)

I've realized that running is a metaphor for my life. (Of course I figured all this out while I was running.) You're alone when you run, yet you're surrounded by people most of the time. But they can't run the run for you. No matter how much support we have, we have to do it on our own.

And there's no perfect run, either. Like there's no perfect life. My runs mimic my days: they're never exactly perfect, but some are as close as they can be. Some runs are epic, just like some days are, and those are the ones we live for.

I run in the ice, the snow, the rain, the heat, and everything in between. Just like I get up and move forward every day, whether it's raining, snowing, or scorching (you get the idea).

I run races I know I could never win, but I do it to challenge myself and to break up the status quo. Just like I'm trying (yes, still trying) to learn to play the guitar. I'm not doing it to be Joni Mitchell or running to be Joan Benoit; I'm just doing it to improve the quality of my days. Because whenever we're pushed, we usually respond by pushing back. And I think pushing back is exactly what helps us to keep moving forward.

Running: A Metaphor for Parenting?

Printed October 2009

So I'm running the Tufts 10K last October in Boston with my twelve-year-old daughter, Riley, and as we're taking the first corner onto Charles Street, it hits me: running may just be the perfect metaphor for parenting.

We ran for one hour and six minutes together, just the two of us (minus the eight thousand-plus runners running with us). And the whole race, from start to finish, had earmarks of how we parent our kids all over it.

"Did you remember to tie your shoes?" "Double knots, right?" "How about the bathroom…did you go?" "Lemme help you with that timing chip." "Remember, pinch the Dixie Cup closed at the water stop."

I helped her pick out what to wear, prepped her on the route, told her when to pull back, and helped her keep her pace. I ran alongside her for 6.2 miles from Back Bay to Cambridge and back. I screamed with her under the Longfellow Bridge and pointed out the elites when they ran by us at the turnaround on Memorial Drive. But I couldn't take one step for her. With her, yes. For her, no.

That's what's so symbolic about our life as parents. We give our kids a lifetime of training, but on race day it's all them. We're coaches and trainers, tutors and mentors, but what our job is really about is getting them to the start.

I guess we all evolve into pit crews at some point. We watch every race, we show them where the hazards are, and then we fix the broken chassis when they run off course.

We all watch our kids on the soccer field or the basketball court or the track, but we're on the sidelines. We're onlookers, spectators. It's tough for any of us to feel that feeling they get when they're achieving something firsthand. But I came as close as any parent could to feeling it while we ran. I got a glimpse. I felt her success and her pride. I saw that we can take our kids only so far before we have to (*and we really do have to*) let them take the wheel. It doesn't mean we have to get out of the car; it just means we have to move over and let them drive.

We've got a pretty active family, so we've done a lot together over the years. Typical stuff like bike, ski, snowboard, hike. But few of the things we've done together have left a mark on me as much as running that race together. That day was epic. I feel lucky we had that moment together. She knew I was there if she needed me. But she didn't, which is secretly what we all really want. Or, I think, what we should want.

We do our best as parents to show our kids the way. Sometimes we may go nine miles out of our way to do it, but we still manage to get them there. We want them to follow in our footsteps but at the same time be better than we were. That's why next year I'm hoping *she'll* be pacing *me*.

Let's be Amish for a While

Printed November 2009

I have to be honest, sometimes the idea of being Amish really appeals to me. There's a lot to be said for living the simple life. I guess I've been hypersensitive lately to how much I depend on all the devices in my life, and I'm feeling like I need to take a step back.

I think the Amish might be onto something with this resisting modern conveniences thing. It's kind of a neat idea that if you can't grow it, sew it, or make it, you just don't have it. It's so simple. Can we say that the quality of their lives is better or worse because they don't have smartphones or Wi-Fi? I honestly don't know. I'm sure the Amish would be going over their monthly texting allowance too, if they had the chance. But they don't. I guess you don't miss what you never had. But I'm actually jealous that there are people out there living without Hotmail accounts and streaming video. I'm not saying I want to sell my house and move to Pennsylvania Dutch country; I just feel like technology intrudes a little too far into our lives sometimes.

Don't get me wrong, I'm not denouncing all these sexy little devices that let us check e-mails in the checkout aisle; I appreciate the convenience and the efficiency. I kind of have to by default; my husband works for Microsoft, and bashing this stuff too much would be marital suicide. There just doesn't seem to be a place anymore that we can go to get off-line. And I miss being off-line.

I've been feeling a lot lately like we all need to roll things back to a time when people used to have to actually get off the couch to change the channel. Back to when fans at rock concerts lit Bic lighter for an encore instead of holding up their cell phone display screen. Everything is so automated and hot-wired now that there's no such thing anymore as doing it the old-fashioned way.

I'm conflicted, though, because I really do understand technology's usefulness in medicine and education, banking and communication. And God knows, as a mom I value it for connectivity and safety. I'd never give up being able to stay connected with my kids 24-7. I just worry that with everyone plugged into a different device, we're not connecting enough with each other anymore.

Talk to my husband, the consummate geek, and he'll tell you that he could never be as accessible as a husband and father without mobile devices. When we're road tripping somewhere with our kids and I'm wishing the car could be a refuge from outside contact so we can all just connect, Dave's telling me to look at all the work he can do while we're together. And I get that. I guess it all depends on your point of view. When it's your passion or your livelihood, all these gadgets help you maintain a healthy work/life balance. But when you're looking for a way to disconnect, they're just an intrusion.

I'm not saying we should dump all our MP3 players and net books in a landfill; I'm just saying that I think we could all benefit from unplugging every once in a while, just so we can remember what thinking and doing for ourselves feels like. (Plus, it gives our batteries a chance to recharge.)

Why We Owe Abe Lincoln a Drumstick

Printed November 2009

Abe Lincoln was a genius. And not even for the obvious reasons why people considered him great. Sure, he was the guy who gave us the Emancipation Proclamation and the Homestead Act (definitely great, no doubt), but did you know he was also the guy who gave us Thanksgiving? And boy, do we owe him one!

It was Lincoln who actually made it a nationally observed holiday in 1863. And do you know why he did it? (This is the genius part.) It was the Civil War era and times were about as tough as times get, so he did it to brighten peoples' spirits. He created a diversion so that people could refocus. Super smart guy.

Now I'm not suggesting that the bad year we've all had can be compared to what our forefathers went through during the Civil War, but it's definitely been a rough ride. The American Dream hasn't been very dreamy lately, and people are feeling battered and tired. Between the piss-poor economy and H1N1, we're getting picked off like ducks in open water. There isn't one of us who doesn't know someone who's lost a job, been demoted, or filed for Chapter 11. And if you don't, then you know someone with swine flu.

Everyone's had it rough, and we could all use a distraction. But I think we need more than just a day off to catch up on sleep. I think we need the day to spend a little time giving thanks for how good we still have it. Because we can all sometimes be a little too guilty of focusing on what we *don't* have instead of what's right in front of us. After all, Thanksgiving was designed to make us stop, look, and listen to what we've still got in spite of everything else that might be going wrong.

So forget about the ritual part of the holiday for a minute (like the Macy's Day Parade and all the football) and just think about the day. Everything stops and we just gather. Whatever else may be happening on the periphery, it stays on the periphery for that one day. We spend the day with the people who mean the most: our family and our friends (who might as well be family). And we eat. And we drink. And we repeat. And no matter what's gone on the day before or what's going to happen the day after, we enjoy the day. And we should because that's what Lincoln knew we needed. And we still need it now almost 150 years later.

So when you're sitting down to serve or be served this Thanksgiving, say thanks twice: once for what you've got sitting around your table, and again to your buddy Abe for knowing that tryptophan works a helluva lot better than Tamiflu to cure what ails us.

There's No Such Thing as Small Change

Printed December 2009

So I found this stat in *The New York Times* online that says a third of us will break our New Year's resolutions by the end of January. A third. By the end of January. Well, that's depressing. But don't worry; I think I know why and how we can change it.

New Year's is the end and the beginning all at the same time, so naturally it's the perfect time to make changes. It's the end of the year so we're all a little antsy and ready for a change. We're all super-motivated to start fresh and clean the slate. So most of us give in to that natural impulse and take a good, long (and sometimes painful) look at ourselves. Then we figure out what we can do better. And that's good. We're supposed to do that; it's human nature.

Unfortunately most of us want to change so much so fast that we end up ripping ourselves down to the studs and have no idea how to move forward. We want to be skinny, emotionally stable, nonsmoking, professionally driven überparents overnight. And that's why we burn out so fast. We set these totally unrealistic goals for ourselves, and then we collapse under the weight of them.

We're all so hung up on fixing everything (and doing it yesterday) that we forget that we can't, that we're not supposed to. Change takes time and commitment. But our culture has this affinity for instant gratification and this propensity toward perfectionism. So without even realizing it, we're constantly contradicting the old to-err-is-human and patience-is-a-virtue ideas. We forget that we're *supposed* to screw up and we're *supposed* to take our time. Because if we were all supposed to be perfect, we'd be prewired that way.

And I'm probably guiltier of this than anyone I know. That's why this year I'm switching it up and I'm going to let myself screw up and I'm going to take my time doing it. I'm going to whittle my goals down and pick a few good ones. I'm going to minimize in order to maximize. And I'm going to plod along and take my time. And if everything isn't perfect, well, then I guess to err is human, right?

We've become a society that expects that we can do everything instantaneously. We're no longer driven by the process; we're driven by the result. People don't seem as willing anymore to follow a path to get where they want to go—they just want to be airlifted to the end. The trouble is, they're missing the journey.

I'm not sure who came up with this, but it's brilliant and it's my slogan for 2010: "There's no such thing as small change." Feel free to try it on too, and see it if fits.

Timing Really Might Be Everything

Printed January 2010

The older I get, the more I realize that life is all about timing. I know this is a pretty simple and obvious idea, but it's amazingly true when you really think about it. Things just seem to have a much bigger impact on us when we're open and ready for them. Things like getting married and having kids, losing weight, or writing a newspaper column. They're all more meaningful when you're ready and the timing is right.

Friendships are like that, too. They're affected by chemistry for sure, but even more by simple timing. People come and go in our lives for so many different reasons, and if you stop and think about why you're friends with certain people at certain times, it usually makes perfect sense. And there are umpteen different kinds of friends, depending on what period of life we're talking about: the playgroup friends from when your kids were little, work friends, prekid friends, basketball league and book club friends. Some come and then go while others stay pretty constant. Then there are those who bounce in and out at different points. Yet all are influenced by the timing of when they occur. All are valuable, even the negative ones. All have meaning. And all of them help define who we are.

I can think back over dozens of friendships I've had over the years that seemed like they'd go the distance, and for no other reason than timing, they just slipped away. Maybe someone moved or your kids changed schools or you ski every weekend so you're not around as much. It's not necessarily that the feelings changed, it's just that the timing was off. The irony is, hardly any ended badly; they just took on a different feel. And I think that's just what happens.

It's those cyclical friendships, though, that have really been on my mind lately. You know, the ones that are like vintage clothes: they always seems to come back around and fit just right at different times. Maybe that's because the vintage stuff is crafted differently, like our oldest friendships. They're bound together in a different way. If you think about it, most of the old stuff we all have lying around tends to outlast the new stuff. Not because the new stuff isn't good but because the old stuff is made a different way. The old stuff is forged differently, so it's got different durability.

I think in some way we all lament the changing of our friendships, especially the ones that seem to have faded. But I don't think we should. I think we should appreciate that things happen for a reason and exactly when they're supposed to and that the history and emotions that bind us to people endures. So don't write off those jazz shoes from high school just yet...they'll probably be back.

Are We Too Paranoid?

Printed March 2010

So my two daughters (nine and twelve) are out walking our dog around the neighborhood last weekend, and a seemingly harmless retiree-age man says "hi" to them. He doesn't rush at them or, God forbid, try to pull them into a windowless van; he just says "hi." They say "hi" back. Keep in mind, though, he's alone—no dog, no kids, nothing—and they don't recognize him. He starts chatting with them about how much he loves dogs, tells them a cute dog story, and then after a few minutes, they go their separate ways.

After my kids get home, and while my youngest is ripping into a bag of Pirate's Booty, she offhandedly tells me about "this guy" who chatted them up on their walk.

Hang on a sec…what did she say?!

Did she say that some guy walking alone whom they didn't know stopped them and started talking to them? Simultaneously one half of my brain starts thinking, "Aw, how sweet; people can be so nice," while the other half is ready to call in a police sketch artist to do a composite. It's right about this point when I pulled my husband into the conversation just to make sure I wasn't being a completely paranoid lunatic. He agreed that it was a total red flag and that I wasn't just being a freak show.

So we talked with our kids, as we so often do, about being wary of strangers and about how the majority of people are genuinely good. But there are still those deviants out there who buy puppies and carry a bag of Twizzlers just to prey on unsuspecting kids.

I hate that it doesn't feel normal anymore for someone to be innocuously nice. In fact, it crushes me since I'm not a skeptic by nature. I'm the naïve one who always believes that the panhandler you just gave five bucks to won't cash it in for a Seagram's nip. But I feel like our generation has been conditioned to worry about everything and everyone.

Back in the seventies and eighties when I was a kid, we had the "don't-talk-to-strangers" and "don't-cross-your-eyes-or-they'll-stay-that-way" isms. Our parents definitely warned us in their way. The difference is I feel like my generation talks with our kids about everyday threats almost as often as we fill up the car. So it's when I catch myself being too paranoid that I realize I need to be consciously aware of letting my kids think for themselves and use the skills and common sense we've given them. After all, this is their world now, and they need to figure out how to live in it. Sure, it's our responsibility to protect and empower our kids, but we have to learn to resist the urge to be "helicopter parents," constantly hovering over them.

The worst thing we can do is become a generation of "overparenters" because all that will do is create a new generation of nut jobs.

I recognize that things are different now. I'm just not willing to admit that things are worse. If anything, I think times are pretty relative. I know we've got sexting, Internet predators, cyber bullies, and teen sex. So there's a lot to legitimately be edgy about. Back in the seventies we had wrist rockets, dolls with actual, swallowable button eyes, and Pop Rocks (and those things were lethal, right?). But we survived.

It's true that this isn't the same world that my generation grew up in. Who knew anyone growing up who had nut allergies? Who wore a bike helmet or packed an egg salad sandwich with a freezer pack? Who knew from air bags or antilock brakes or PG-13?

The good news is that in spite of it all, the crime rate in this country has been quietly dropping. According to the FBI's preliminary numbers for 2009, law enforcement agencies throughout the US reported a decrease of 4.4 percent in the number of violent crimes. So that should be a good litmus test that we can loosen up a little.

Maybe if we show more confidence in ourselves as parents and rely on the strength of the wisdom and support we give our kids, we can give them the right to succeed and fail on their own. They've earned it. Because if we keep them in bubble wrap for too long, they're just going to shatter the minute they hit the ground on their own.

Oh yeah, did I forget to mention that my twelve-year-old ended up telling me that she had her hand on her cell phone in her pocket while the stranger was talking to them? Apparently she was keeping track of how long they were talking and of what she would do to keep herself and her sister safe if something happened.

Well, whaddya know?

Life is Like a Game of Boggle

Printed April 2010

So here's a thought: Imagine inventing a catch phrase. Something no one's ever said. It's gotta feel amazing, right? Like the SportsCenter guy who came up with "Cool as the other side of the pillow." He was the first. *The first*. Like Neil Armstrong being the first guy *ever* to stand on the moon. Just imagine it.

Well, that's my dream. And since I always tell my kids to dream big, I'm going for it…

If Forrest Gump's momma can say, "Life is like a box of choco-lates," then I don't feel too quirky saying I think life is even *more* like a game of Boggle. Just give it time and it'll be even bigger than "If life gives you lemons, make lemonade."

I know this all sounds like a reach, but I want you to know that I didn't just randomly start thinking about this Boggle thing in the eight-items-or-less line at Crosby's. I actually had a death in the fam-ily last month, and it was such a powerful experience for me that it made it strikingly clear how uniquely we all experience life. In exactly the same way we play Boggle.

You know the game—it's the one with the three-minute egg timer and the tray of plastic alphabet cubes. Hasn't changed since the early seventies. It's got a simple point: make as many different words as you can in three minutes.

But what makes it so unique, , is that even though we're all using the same letters, we're all seeing them from different angles and putting them together in different ways. I've played with a whole group of people and not one of us had the same word. It's uncanny.

This simple little game epitomizes, in almost every way, how differently we all see the same life we're living. Granted, we all have unique nuances to our lives that make our circumstances different from the next guy. But we're all living under the same roof, so to speak, and we've all got the basics like health, family, work, money, and love that are pretty common denominators. So let's put it this way, we've all got enough of the same stuff going on that I think it's fair to say that we're all playing off the same "board."

See, we're big Boggle players in my family. Big. Huge. So the game is a really easy thing for me to relate with. Pair that with the fact that I've always connected with things in a more visual way than a theoretical one, and you've got the perfect analogy. At least for me. (And for my Boggle-happy husband, Dave, who thought this idea would make the best column ever.)

It was while I watched my mother's older brother, my uncle Jay, die in hospice last month that the idea occurred to me. Strange timing, I know, but hospice lends itself to a lot of downtime, and most of that is spent inside your own head. And since my family tends to travel in packs, it wasn't too surprising to see at least ten of us in my uncle's hospital room at any given time. Each one of us watching him die.

I know this sounds morbid, but you have to trust me and hang in there.

Even though we were all watching the same thing, we were all seeing something very different. Some of us saw my uncle's dying as a relief, a way for him to be at peace from the pain, while others saw it as a devastating loss. Some cried bitterly while the rest of us laughed uncontrollably, and some just reflected. We were all playing off the same game tray, and yet the way we each played was so different.

The connection to the game seemed so obvious because in Boggle, like life, we're all playing on the same board at the same time with the same pieces, but we all see the board in a completely different way. Four different people may be playing off the same sixteen letters, but they all come up with a completely different list of words.

After all, life is all about the way we perceive and react to things.

For instance, while my husband might think that jumping out of a perfectly good airplane is insane, I might think it's the most awesome thing ever.

Take this season's opening day at Fenway. It's a simple and straightforward example of what I mean. There was the Red Sox perspective and (hack, hack, hack, excuse me) the Yankee perspective. A nine-seven win by Boston means it's Miller Time on Yawkey Way. While a seven-nine loss by New York means a depressing Monday in Manhattan.

It all depends on which side of the board you're on.

An Ode to Mister Rogers

Printed May 2010

I'm in love with Mister Rogers.
OK. There. I said it.

Not the I-want-to-throw-him-on-the-kitchen-table kind of love. (Although that red-zipper cardigan was pretty hot.) What I'm talking about is more of a love and respect of his "way" than of the hunk of a man he was in those sexy canvas boat sneakers.

I'm not admitting that I drive around town singing, "It's a beautiful day in the neighborhood," because then I'd lose all credibility. (I actually just think it in my head, which really doesn't count.) What I will say, though, is that it was plain-Jane Fred Rogers who taught me this: *we way undervalue the simple, little day-to-day things in life.*

I think we all have the tendency to think of the little, repetitive things we do every day as monotonous, but we shouldn't. We should think of them more like we think of comfort food—the things we depend on to be the stabilizers in our life and settle us when we get rattled. You know, the things that create a sense of normalcy and routine. Things like grocery shopping and dropping off the dry cleaning and taking our kids to and from school are the little anchors that keep us from floating out into open water. In the same way that when we're stressed we reach for things that soothe us like deep-fried Twinkies (but they're only used in case of a real emotional emergency.)

And Mister Rogers was the master of simplicity and routine. Every day it was the same thing—a lot like watching Bill Murray endlessly repeat the same day in *Groundhog Day*. The way Mister Rogers walked through the door every afternoon and traded the coat for the cardigan and the loafers for the Sperrys. He did the same things the same way every day. And in doing that he gave us things we could always count on, and that equals security. And we all crave that on some level. That's why I love him.

He proved every day that there's comfort in routine. And no one loves routine more than me. Just ask my husband, Dave; he'll tell you. Although he'll probably tell you that he thinks I'm just outside the crosshairs of normal because I love the mundaneness of life so much. But I can't help it. I do. He'd definitely tell you that I actually do come home every afternoon and trade my clogs for my old, nappy, fake Ugg slippers and an eggplant hoodie cardigan (buttons, though, no zipper). He'd also make fun of how I love the morning drive down Atlantic Avenue when I'm taking the kids to school. I love passing the same people in the same spot every day, holding the same green Fiestaware mug, and waving to people I know who are doing exactly the same thing. I can tell you exactly where I'll pass Amanda or Janet or Judy or Steve and at exactly which point on my drive my coffee will turn ice cold. But I love it because it grounds me to my life.

In his uncomplicated and unassuming way, Mister Rogers glorified the beauty of consistency. He showed us every day that the little routine things aren't really as mundane as we think they are because there's comfort in routine.

The ordinary little things we have to do every day have incredible value and purpose. And Fred Rogers, in his own unique little way, made the inconsequential seem consequential.

And because of it, he could be my neighbor anytime.

Extending Our Warranty

Printed June 2010

I've always figured that if we treat our bodies like we treat our cars, we should get a good few hundred thousand miles out of them. A lube here, a knee replacement there, and you can keep just about anything running.

You've seen the Toyota ads with the Corolla that still runs like new after 595,000 miles. We should be able to apply the same philosophy to our bodies, shouldn't we? I mean look at Jack LaLanne. What's he now, 150? And the guy's still knocking off two hundred knuckle-ups a day.

The way I see it, if we just take care of our stuff it should last. Bodies included. But it takes some follow-through.

I guess I'm thinking about this a lot more lately because I seem to have way too many things to tell my chiropractor to fix whenever I see him. And that freaked me out for a while, until I came to the conclusion that this aging thing will happen in spite of us. So why not embrace it?

Clearly the older we get, the more important it becomes to just keep moving forward. It's that whole inertia idea: objects in motion remain in motion. So the more we keep moving, the better off we'll be.

I do think we all hit our own threshold where things just start to sputter and stall a little, but I think that just means we have to make more of an obvious effort to keep things running. So instead of putting off our dental checkup for two years (sorry, Dr. Baratz, those couple of years totally slipped by Dave), we actually need to go. The mammograms. The annual physicals. All of it.

I think people have this incredible misconception once we round our 40s; it's like the day after your car warranty expires when parts start falling off in the middle of the road, and the next thing you know you're hitchhiking home carrying your front bumper.

I hate to be the one to break it to you, but this aging thing happens, whether we want it to or not; it just depends on how we handle it. Just look at metabolisms. Can any of us eat the same way we did in college and still close our button fly? Uh, no. Just ask my husband, Dave, who used to eat a big beef with ketchup from Mino's, onion rings, and a vanilla milk shake at least three times a week when we were in high school. Now he's got to run about a thousand miles a week just to digest a clam roll from Woodman's once a year. And I don't even want to discuss what I can't eat anymore. So don't ask. The point is we need to tweak things a little as we go. Eat a little less and walk a few extra miles. Problem solved. It's really not that hard. We really don't need complete reconstruction when things start to sag. It's called gravity and inevitability.

You've got to keep in mind that "you get what you get, and you don't get upset." If you're overweight, stack the deck in your favor and go join a gym; if you hate your hair, get some highlights; if you're not flexible, do some yoga. There are always options. And they don't have to be extreme ones.

Stiff joints aren't a signal that we should head straight for the elephant graveyard; it just means we need to switch things up a little and try something different. It may take us a little longer to get where we're going, but it doesn't mean we're out of gas.

I really do think aging is way more in our head than we think. Attitude goes a long way. If you're convinced that just because your cartilage is shrinking a little you're one step away from assisted living, well then, I guess you're done. But if you embrace the fact that our aches and pains and varicose veins are just mile markers, you can just do your best to accept them and work with what you've got.

Remember, a little duct tape and some WD-40 goes a long way.

It's Nice to be Nice to the Nice

Printed July 2010

As far as I know, no one's ever called me pretentious or pompous or shallow or conceited (at least not to my face). But what I'm now ready to publicly admit is that I am a snob. And I know it—only not in the way you might think. And I'm not going to hide it anymore.

But I'm also very unique in my snobbiness.

That's because I'm a new breed of snob. So new, in fact, that you're hearing the term right here for the very first time.

I'm a courtesy snob. And damn proud of it.

I'm old fashioned; I believe that a hello begets a hello back. Wave, nod, wink, flinch, blow me a kiss, I don't care. Just acknowledge me when I reach out to you—for no other reason than it's the right thing to do.

Would you go to someone's house for dinner without bringing a bottle of wine or some molasses cookies? God, I hope not. Then how are there so many people who can completely ignore a wave, a held-open door, or a simple hello? I just don't get it.

Maybe it just seems so obvious around here because there are 20,000 of us jammed into 19 square miles on this tiny peninsula. But I know that the more I see it, the more deeply it roots me in my snobbiness.

I'm a simple girl. I believe in easy, straightforward ideas like do unto others, practice what you preach, and never bite the hand that feeds you. And it's nice to be nice to the nice. I say it constantly. It's probably the most heard idiom in my house. Just ask my kids.

(I admit, I'm a little bit of an idioms queen, and I hear myself saying that one an awful lot lately.)

So simple, this idea of civility. So why is it such a struggle for so many people?

This acknowledgment of niceties seems like it should be a pretty straightforward thing. So I just don't get why more people aren't wired for it.

I don't think I'm wrong or unfair to always expect a thank-you wave or some kind of general acknowledgment of basic social courtesies. Someone lets you cross the street, so you wave. Someone lets you merge into traffic; you smile. Someone holds the door for you at Shubie's; you say thanks. Someone waves to you when they run by you on the causeway, and you should wave back (or at least nod; running takes a lot of energy, so I'm willing to compromise on this one).

Simple gesticulation, that's all it is. It should be jackhammered into our DNA from birth, and yet too many people can't seem to do it. I'm just saying that if someone makes the effort, make the effort back. Simple acknowledgment goes a long way, not to mention the fact that it's just plain courteous.

And what cracks me up the most is that reciprocity, in any form, just makes you feel good. It's like the whole it's-better-to-give-than-to-receive thing. So what the heck?

I'm not saying people should be expected to be in a good mood, waving and whistling out their Volvo windows 24-7. Plus, we don't have eyes in the back of our heads, so it's expected that we're going to miss some stuff. But considering how much isn't working in the world (hunger, poverty, homelessness, war), wouldn't it be nice to at least be nice to each other while everything around us goes to hell?

So let's try a little social experiment. Let's make Marblehead the birthplace of the It's-Nice-to-Be-Nice-to-the-Nice Movement. There's no overhead, no storefront, no marketing cost. It's cheap and easy. In fact, I'll even throw in a personal guarantee that if you're nice to someone, they'll be nice back. I guaaaaaraaaaaannnteee it. Think of it this way: it can't hurt, it doesn't cost, and it'll probably add years to your life because you'll be so giddy all the time from everyone being so nice.

So when this takes off and really puts Marblehead on the map (way more than that whole birthplace-of-the-American-navy thing), remember where you heard the idea first, OK? Then you can give me a big, fat thank-you wave.

Hurry Up and Wait

Printed July 2010

So I'm in the checkout line at the market last week and the girl behind the register runs out of change.

No big deal.

Or so I thought.

She's perfectly lovely about it, too. Apologizes and says it'll only be a second. And it really *does* only take about thirty-two seconds. But it's what happened during those thirty-two seconds that really threw me.

It's the woman directly behind me. As soon as she gets wind that there's a holdup, the heavy breathing starts. You know, the big audible sighs. Then she starts rearranging her groceries on the belt, pushing them closer to the scanner as if they'll pass through quicker by osmosis. And this is all in the first eight seconds.

Then I hear her draw in a breath and at the same time I hold mine just waiting for it. You know, like when you hear a car screech and you wait for the impact. And then it came. The "Ohhhhhh, come ooooooooon!!!!!!!!!"

Now this woman had to be pushing at least sixty, so she's been at this whole life thing for a while. Which is exactly why she doesn't get a free pass just because she's an AARP member. If anything, she's old enough to know better.

That kind of impatience is just plain wrong. And it irks me. A lot. Most people (age notwithstanding) can manage a little tolerance. Or, at the very least, can control their craziness long enough to get to their car where they can scream it out in private.

Back to the market.

The clock is still ticking here, and the line still hasn't moved.

I've only got like four items, I'm paying in cash, and I've got a reusable bag. So once the cashier is locked and loaded, I'm in/out. But I have to be honest, once that groan hit the air, all bets were off. I was going to count out my nine-dollar-and-seventy-two cent bill in all pennies. And slowly. Just to make a point. (Sometimes tough love is the only way.)

Let's be clear, I don't consider myself an activist by nature (although I did go to a No-Nukes rally with my Aunt Charlotte back in the seventies, and I was only nine), but I do think that certain messages need to be sent to certain people at certain times in certain ways. And there's no better message-sending tool than subtlety. When used correctly, subtlety can hit you like a brick in the face without you ever seeing it coming.

With two kids and a husband, a house, a job, a beagle, a fish, and everything that that implies, I've always got somewhere else I need to be, so time is kind of a commodity. *But not that day.* That day I took my sweet time, and I did it to send a simple message: hurry up and wait, honey.

It makes me sad that there are people out there who can't be even a little patient. It seems like such a straightforward idea, but some people just can't seem to get their minds around it. We all have moments of complete self-absorption, for sure, but overall people should eventually accept the fact that there are 6,826,300,000 of us waiting our turns for something, somewhere, every minute of every day. And that's a helluva line.

I've just seen this attitude way too much lately. And I just wish someone could tell me why. I see it in the car on my way to and from school pickup. I see it in the dumbest places like waiting for treadmills in the gym and at traffic lights. I see it at doctor's offices and in the passing lane on Route 128. I see it at ATMs and restaurants. I see it everywhere. And all for what?

Everybody's jockeying for position just to get somewhere four seconds sooner than the person behind them. Seriously?

I don't think people realize that this low-level impatience is just the first step on the crazy train toward fanaticism. These traits start small and then mushroom out of control. One minute you're cutting someone off in the YMCAparking lot to make it to Tae Bo, and the next minute you're swiping a woman's leg at Crosby's to get the last box of Lucky Charms.

We're not on the Upper West Side. This is Marblehead, remember?

When I was a kid, my aunt Lora down in Warner Robins, Georgia, once told me, "Baby girl, there's no such thing as wasted time. Every minute has a purpose. You can be standing in line at the bank and you can be thinking about what you're going to make for dinner or who you want for president. All that extra time is worthwhile. It just depends on how you use it."

I never forgot that.

So whenever I catch myself getting antsy or impatient, I try to remember that life is way too short as it is. And that's one thing I want to take my sweet time with.

Quit Keeping Up with the Joneses.
They're broke!

Printed August 2010

Generally speaking, I usually try to keep a low profile. But I'm not sure that's going to happen after the ink dries on this one.

So while you're reading, remember: this is an opinion column. O-P-I-N-I-O-N. And honestly, who the hell am I anyway?

You'll need to keep one more thing in mind, though. If you decide to read any further, you'll automatically give up your right to complain. It's a lot like when we used to watch *All in the Family* in the seventies—just by tuning in we unconditionally accepted that Archie was going to offend *someone*. We knew it was coming. A lot like drinking the McDonald's coffee even though you knew it was too hot and then suing anyway.

So for the time being, think of me as a cuter version of Archie Bunker and understand that the complaint window is officially closed after this paragraph.

Just read and then think. Then think some more.

Even though I wasn't born at the Mary Alley Hospital, that's where I got the stitches I have on my chin after I fell down the handicap ramp behind the Bell School when I was two. So in my mind I'm only one degree of separation away from being a true Header.

I've lived in Marblehead practically all my life. Grew up on Cornell Road, raised a family here, lived here, worked here—the full monty.

So make no mistake, I love this town and every beautiful, unique little nuance that comes with it. Except one.

The Joneses. I *hate* the Joneses.

And I hate that so many people feel like they need to keep up with them.

They're at every barbecue, cocktail party, dinner party, and get-together. And they're getting people all worked up. And for what? An ocean view? We *all* practically have an ocean view if we live here. We live on a peninsula, for God's sake.

When I was a kid, I was probably too busy biking back and forth to Tent's Corner for penny candy to notice them, but as a parent raising a family in my favorite little town, I notice the Joneses everywhere.

OK, maybe not a physical version of them, just the illusion of them. (It just sounds so much more dramatic when I personify.)

They're smoke and mirrors, those Joneses. An apparition. They're a lot like fashionable gypsies. They're always moving around, and they always leave everyone curious about their next move.

But the simple idea of them is what's causing so many people to give in to all the conspicuous consumption that goes on around here. Way too many people are trying to keep up. No matter what it takes.

And I just have to wonder...why?

Don't misunderstand me, I'm all for the haves buying and doing and building whatever makes them happy; I just wish so many of the have-nots could find a way to be more content with what they *do* have.

There are plenty of hardworking people around here living within their means, and they deserve a lot of credit because that's not easy, especially in a place where people can so easily give in to an overdeveloped sense of social inferiority.

Remember, someone came up with expressions like "the grass is always greener" because it's human nature to crave. We just can't help ourselves sometimes. Hell, I'll be the first to admit that there have been granite countertops and built-in entertainment centers I've wanted in my life. But wanting is one thing. We all want things.

Coveting is another thing altogether. That's taking wanting to a new and dangerous level, and that's how people can get into trouble.

But think about it: there are only ten commandments, and one whole commandment is dedicated to not coveting. For a reason.

So I'm publically outing the Joneses right here and now. Know this: The Joneses are broke! And you will be too if you keep trying to keep up. I'm just weary of seeing people try so hard to keep up with an illusion, and I think the quality of so many peoples' lives will radically improve if they could just stop looking outward and started looking inward.

Why am I saying any of this? Simple. Because I write about things I see. And I see this everywhere. I hear about it, too, constantly. It's certainly not relegated to just Marblehead, but since I don't write for *The Denver Post*, here I am. And Marblehead's what I know best.

Happiness is relative to who we are, what we have, and what we need. And I just think the baseline of what we all really need to be happy tends to get skewed by what's around us.

Earlier this summer I read an article by New York City freelance writer Martha McPhee where she talks about how much of the quality of her life she felt she lost by trying to keep up with the Joneses. She talked about how she acted "as she thought she should act and wasn't authentic to who she was or what she wanted to be." Then she talked about how she changed herself and the quality of her life simply by letting go of all the preconceptions of what she *thought* would make her happy and concentrated instead on what she already had. It changed everything.

The last line in her article was a Latin phrase that she saw stenciled on a friend's wall: "Omnia quae cupio iam habeo." Everything I want I already have. Now a version of that, in the form of a sign, is hanging on my dining room wall because I don't want to forget it.

Think about it, and then take the Joneses off your speed dial.

There Should be a Road Test for Parenting

Printed September 2010

When you think *sage*, you probably think philosopher or thinker—guys like Confucius or Mencius or Descartes.

You're probably not thinking Keanu Reeves right out of the gate. And I don't blame you. He's not exactly your sagely, wise-man type. Surfer guy or Internet vigilante, sure. Guru, no.

But I tend to look for and appreciate wisdom from more unconventional places. Probably because I feel like the more abstract the wisdom, the more profound and meaningful it's likely to be. And in Ron Howard's 1989 comedy *Parenthood*, I found some of the deepest and most poignant thinking on parenthood I've ever heard. I also found my Confucius. And I call him Keanu.

Dying to know what he said?

Patience, grasshoppa.

People mystify me. They really do. And I'm sure I mystify my share of people, too, in my own quirky way. But since I'm the one typing, we're talking about everyone else *but* me.

I'm especially confused by so many of the people who call themselves parents but really act nothing whatsoever like actual parents.

It's a lot like people in business who manage other people. You've got your good managers, the ones who are flexible, supportive, approachable, and legitimately hard working. And then you've got your slackers, the ones who push papers around their desk all day and always seem like they're moving down the hall with a purpose but are actually moving without any purpose at all.

See where I'm going here?

I'm all for diversity, especially in parenting styles. In fact, I celebrate it. The more unique we are the better. We need uniqueness desperately. I'm not into a cookie-cutter-type world or cookie-cutter-type parenting. Never have been. But, and this is a big but, there *are* things that I think should just naturally have some commonalities, no matter what. Oh, I don't know, things like supervision, presence, interaction, spending time with your kids, and actually nurturing them. These sound reasonable, right? So why do I look around and not see enough of that? I mean, I see it but sparsely. And that's not good.

Since I spend most of my time being a parent or being around them, I tend to be hyperaware of how differently we all do the job. And let me tell you, all parents are definitely *not* created equal.

Here's a perfect example: We're on a family cruise, and every night we watched parents dropping off their cockeyed, hysterical eight-year-old kids at day care at eleven o'clock at night asking how late they could pick them up. (It's 2:30 a.m., in case you were curious.) This is, of course, so they can go to the bar, get trashed, and then gamble away all their spending money.

It's stuff like that that I just can't shake.

I thought the basic idea behind having kids was to raise them. Raise them however you want, I really don't care. Just actually raise them. Having them just isn't enough. That doesn't count. (Well, of course it counts, just not for the purpose of what I'm trying to say.) It's not supposed to be easy. Actively bringing kids up is another job altogether. But isn't that the point?

You've heard of labor of love, right?

A wise Keanu once said that you need a license to buy a dog, to drive a car, even to catch a fish...but they'll let any !#&^$@%$*%@$ be a parent.

And just look around and you can't deny it.

To this day, over twenty years after he said that line, I've never heard anything more insightful or perceptive about parenting.

It's just plain disturbing that almost any idiot with a decent sperm or egg count can be a parent with no written exam or road test required. You have to be fourteen to work. You have to be sixteen to drive. Eighteen to vote. Twenty-one to drink. But there's no test or form or course you need to take to be a parent. Is it me or does it seem a little bass-ackward?

We have to be screened and tested for every major modern right and privilege, yet any moron can have a kid. This, considering that the act of parenting is the oldest and most sacred right in the book. It's just a damn shame that there are so many people out there who don't get that having children is a privilege, not a right.

So here's what I'm suggesting: There should be a road test for parenting. Not sure how exactly to get that one done, but you get what I'm saying. And I'm definitely open to suggestions. Maybe it can be a partnership between the Registry of Motor Vehicles and the Department of Social Services. Who knows? I wish I had a bona fide plan, but I don't. All I can do is put the idea out there and hope that someone bites.

All right, fine, it's not going to happen. I know that. But maybe the simple idea will make the crummy parents out there think better of being so crummy.

Maybe they'll even watch *Parenthood* and learn that when we screw up, our "screwed-up-ness" proves that we care.

And that's worth something, isn't it?

Walk a While in Someone Else's Cast

Printed October 2010

It's amazing the kind of perspective you get from immobility. We're all so used to moving at 100 mph that we never really give much consideration to how we'd manage day to day if we suddenly couldn't get around. And when you factor a couple of kids into the mix, you've got yourself one giant pickle.

Most of us are out there flying from drop-off to pickup with a forty-two stops in between, so we don't have time to think about how we'd get things done if we were suddenly strapped into a boot cast, thrown onto a pair of crutches, and told not to even *think* about climbing stairs without hopping.

Trust me, spend a little time not being able to get around the way you're used to, and all of a sudden everything changes. And whoa, does it change.

We go from sixty to zero with nothing in between, and that's a real awakening. And not the good kind. Which is exactly what I did two weeks ago.

I ended up in a boot cast, on crutches, and with a disproportionately large "good" quad. An experience that you really can't appreciate unless you've spent any real time in a Reebok-Pump-style cast with an order of crutches on the side.

So in the interest of giving you a really good sense of what this implies, let's play a little visualization game:

Get into your imaginary boot cast and grab your make-believe crutches and let's try something simple since you're new at this. (At this point I'm considered a professional now that I'm in my second full week of crutching.)

Let's drive to the market to buy some flowers. And remember, always keep your fractured ankle off the ground whenever you're standing, or your kids will rat on you like Judas giving up Jesus.

First, take off your cast to get in your car, then stow your crutches, and slip into your other shoe (oops, forgot the shoe, have to go back in the house). OK, shoe's on. Drive to the market, put your cast back on, hop to the trunk to get your crutches, throw on your backpack, and get to the flower case. Now put the bouquet between your teeth, back out of the freezer, and get in line. Pay, then beg someone to carry your now-crushed flowers out to your car, and repeat the whole cast on/off process. And this is only errand number one. This pared-down version of my day is only about a half of the stops I usually make. But the length of my day is still the same. It takes me the same amount of time to get half as much done. And this is all without my leg ever touching the ground (at least in theory).

Forget about doing a full food shop. Not happening. Already tried and it was laughable. No dog walking. No umbrella holding. Definitely no getting the milk out of the fridge and over to the counter. (Calcium is grossly overrated anyway and clearly was no help to my bones whatsoever). And I'm not even going to broach the whole stair subject. Let's just say this, if you can only use one leg and you have to hold your crutches, then climbing stairs becomes a conundrum. It's just impossible to figure it out.

I'm exhausted even writing about it. How are you doing?

I've only been at this for two weeks, and I've acquired such a deep respect for anyone who does this on a regular basis.

Growing up, two of my cousins used walkers or crutches, and I never fully got it until now. And this was every day for life. So my teeny, tiny, little glimpse into a world with real limitations is pretty damn sobering.

Being immobile for a while helped me see how much we take the simple, everyday things for granted. I just wish it didn't take traumatic events to change our perspectives so much. Which is why I'm almost inclined to tell everyone to go out and put themselves in a boot cast for a week just for the helluvit, for clarity's sake.

I wish there was a way we could all maintain a sense of appreciation on the off days, when things aren't upside down and difficult. But I guess that's human nature. We get comfortable and take things for granted without even realizing we're doing it. As soon as a crisis is over, we're back to business as usual, and we forget how good we've got it.

I'm sure your average day looks an awful lot like mine, getting into and out of the car at least twenty-five times. School drop-off, home, work, Crosby's, Starbucks, the ATM, the cleaner, back to Crosby's (forgot bread), Chet's (forgot, again, to return our DVD), the gas station, CVS, school pickup, back home, soccer practice #1, home again (forgot shin guards), soccer practice #2, Fen Yang for takeout, home. Sounding familiar?

OK, it's really not *that* bad. I'm just exaggerating for the dramatic effect because it reads better.

But for most of us, this is our way of life, and we don't think twice about it. Generally. Yeah, sure, there are the days when it gets a little ridiculous and you realize that you've been in the car more than you've been in your house. To most of us, though, our schedules are a force of habit, and we completely take for granted that we can get to and from all these places. Until one day when something happens and we can't.

But since I'm a big believer in mixing things up every once in a while for perspective's sake, I'm trying to look at this in a positive way.

There's a negative side here, for sure. First, you really *do* need a cabana boy when you can't get around. Mine's name is Dave. And lucky for me he took me for better, worse, and even slightly broken because I'd be lost without him.

Because you really can't do it all alone.

Second, for every five minutes it normally takes me to do something, I need to add an extra five on the front and the back. So, now, it basically takes me forty-eight hours to do a full day's worth of stuff. That means lots of planning ahead. Everything gets mapped out in the most logical possible sequence to avoid backtracking. Backtracking on crutches is bad. It's also become very clear very quickly that you absolutely cannot food shop on crutches. Except for gum (just not the jumbo packs because they throw off your center of gravity). Unless you have a Dave, you use Peapod or it just doesn't happen. I've also learned that a new physics law needs to be invented as soon as possible that would allow someone to stand on crutches with one leg bent and bring a pot of boiling water from the stove across the kitchen to the sink. (Newton's physics law really needs to be tweaked.)

But there's also a yin to all that yang. The positive side is that you get a real, true appreciation for how easy most of us have it. And you look at anyone who doesn't have it as easy in a completely different way. And we need that. We all need that. Because most people have limitations. Some are visible, some aren't.

Once you stop everything changes. Once you're forced to give up the things you take for granted, you start seeing things differently. And the more time I spend in this wretched plastic cast, the more I realize that even the most inconvenient things serve a purpose. Anything that compels us to change our vantage point is worthwhile because it allows us to see things in a new and different way.

So when you see me hopping around town on one leg, I'm not just throwing myself into my work and doing all this in the name of journalistic integrity. This is the real deal. And let me tell you, immobility is a humbling experience, for sure. You think it's tough walking in someone else's shoes, try a cast and see how that goes.

For the New Year, Go Big or Go Home

Printed January 2013

So here we are. The ball dropped right on cue, and we got our hard reset. The one we all wait for, sometimes even pray for, when the New Year comes. That magic moment when the switch gets flipped and everybody gets a do-over. A mulligan. A clean slate.

OK, less than two weeks in and what are we supposed to do now?

Now I don't want to harsh your mellow, especially when you've got such good intentions and you're all amped up, but those quirky stats guys say the actual percentage of people who follow through with all their resolutions is shamefully low. So low that the *University of Scranton Journal of Clinical Psychology* says that out of the 45 percent of people who actually *make* resolutions, only 8 percent of those people are actually sticking with them. That's pretty weak. But not to worry, I've been giving this a lot of thought, and I'm pretty sure I've got the whole thing figured out.

We're all capable of change. And we're all certainly capable of great things. I think what's happened is that most people either don't know it or they're too afraid to admit it. People tend to go about change the wrong way, worrying too much about overloading themselves with expectations and commitments, when that's actually exactly what they *should* be doing.

From what I see, there's a real trend nowadays of people keeping the bar low so they don't have to work that hard to clear it. But what

47

they're missing is, the higher they raise the bar, the higher they'll realize they want to go.

That's why I'm convinced that the key to sticking with all of our great intentions and resolutions is simply realizing that we need to quit doing things so piecemeal. Enough of this gradually-putting-our-toe-in-the-water crap. We need to cannonball right into the deep end and then sink or swim.

We need to go big or go home.

It's like the advice my ski buddy Vince used to give me right before we'd drop onto an icy headwall: commit to the fall line, he'd always say. And, as always, Vin was right. Because the more you give in to the natural momentum and force that propels us all forward in life, the more that force will work with you to actually make the trip easier.

Are you still with me?

Look, we're all designed with shoulders for a reason. That's because we're built to bear weight. The problem is our culture has gotten too obsessed with lightening our own load by quick fixes, easy outs, and passing the buck, so we've forgotten that the only real way to accomplish anything anymore is to dig in and work for it. We're meant to push the envelope. Remember, we're at the top of the food chain for a reason. We evolved. And that's because we had to. Life necessitated it. We had to persevere and work for it. We learned to gut it out, sweat it out, and figure it out to really accomplish anything. That's the basis of human nature. We all want to accomplish things, especially when those things involve personal growth, and triumph. Basic human nature has actually never changed; we've just gotten lazy and gotten used to quitting too soon.

If we really, truly want to cook these resolutions through, we need to turn the heat up. Way up. And that's because people have given in to aiming too low. (Smarmy voice here) "Ohhhhhh, I'll just focus on one resolution at a time. Don't want to get too overwhelmed with change." If that's your attitude, you're coming at it from the wrong end of the field. To make big, capital improvements we sometimes need to rip things down to the studs and start from scratch.

So this time, resolve to go big. Or just go home.

Life, Made Easy

Printed March 2013

Iget made fun of a lot. But it's OK; I have a thick skin. I can take it. I'm tough.

It's really just people being playful, I know.

Truth is, I get made fun of—are you ready for this—because I like to be positive. I know, right? Ironic that of all the things people could legitimately bust on me for, that's why I get heckled. But it's just how I'm wired. What can I say?

My mom is actually the happiest person on the planet, so I guess I was genetically predisposed to be happy right from conception. And anyone who knows her is giggling right now, because they know it's true. There's honestly nobody happier than Sandy. So it's in the genes. But you *would not believe* how many people call me out on it. People make cracks about it all the time, almost like I'm a deviant. Cracks me up.

And it got me thinking…

Doesn't it seem a little odd that the person who has a good attitude and likes to spin things in a positive way is the one who gets ragged on? Have happy, positive people really become that much of the moral minority?

I mean, think about it for a sec, doesn't there seem to be a disproportionate number of people out there who actually seem happier when they're unhappy? Who knows, maybe they function better that way. It's like when you're sick—I mean swine flu sick—and somehow moaning makes you feel better. And moaning, when done correctly, is just plain wretched. But the moaner feels better somehow. See what I mean? I guess for some people having something to moan about just gives them a purpose.

Seriously, though, even if the-cup-is-always-half-full kind of happiness is outside your wheelhouse, I truly believe that deep down everyone has the capacity and the fundamental desire to be positive, at least most of the time.

I mean just look at what the Grinch accomplished in only one night. He was a miserable bastard and he had one garden-variety epiphany and *bang*, he turned it all around. So it *can* happen. But happiness, I truly believe, like anything, is a choice—a conscious choice.

And choices are what propel us through the day. Through life. They're what everything we do is based on. We choose to eat right. Or not. We choose to exercise. Or not. We choose to be faithful. Or not. We choose to be nice. Or not. We choose to give the guy who cut us off on Pleasant Street the finger. Or not.

I tell my kids a lot of things on a regular basis. I'm more than a little redundant. God bless their little hearts for putting up with my crazy. And one of the things they hear constantly from me is that I believe we all actually have very little control over most of the stuff in our life. I think we all spend the majority of our time reacting to things and to people. That's why I tell them it's so important to remember that although we really don't have any control over how other people act and react, we *do* have complete control over how we as individuals react to what gets thrown at us. That we *can* control. That we *can* manage. And that, my friends, is a powerful little nugget of truth. And, just between you and me, may actually be the key to happiness. Because once you've got that down, you're driving the bus. You're in complete control.

But it's a commitment, this being positive thing. It takes work and a conscious effort. Then don't most things that are worthwhile? And doesn't a person's overall attitude toward life seem particularly worthwhile, especially when you stack it up against other, slightly less important things like soaps or March Madness? Being positive seems like a pretty legitimate thing to throw yourself into.

Now we all know that I'm really not the only one out there who acts this way. But I do see a definite, obvious pattern of people just not making the effort or the decision to be positive.

Look, Pollyannaism is a real term for a reason (yes, seriously, it's real), because there *are* actually plenty of positive people out there. And I guess I'm calling the issue out because I still see a lot of lazy people who just can't be bothered to think positive, and I don't like it. And because this column is about what I think, I get to say anything I want. When you write a column, you can say anything you want.

There's this local grassroots group called the b Positive Project that I love because these guys believe in nothing more than promoting a positive lifestyle and attitude. They do it with T-shirts and headbands and hats. And they're just one tangible example of how easy it is to send the message that attitude actually *is* everything. Their message is simple but impactful: "The difference between a good day and a bad day is your attitude." And that's all I'm really saying. It's a choice.

Learning to manage the impulse to be negative is just a clear-cut behavior modification. But it's doable. Maybe not an overnighter but well within the acceptable range of achievable for the average person. Just like when we retrain ourselves to stop biting our nails or swearing. It's challenging, and it takes discipline and commitment, but people do it successfully every day just by making a conscious choice to make it happen. I think that some people are actually just afraid to let go of the negativity that holds them back because it's become almost like a crutch that keeps them stable. It's something to hide behind. The irony is, though, if they'd just cut it loose, they'd be happier for it.

So at this point, I'm not even going to broach any of the obvious benefits of staying positive because you're hip to all that. Like you don't need me saying anything about how being positive will help reduce stress, improve coping skills, ease depression, make you more likable. Pffffffffft. You know all this.

Plus, and this has to be reason A-#1 to harness the positive within, no one wants to be around a complainer. People hate that guy. When you're always the one who finds a problem with everyone and everything, watch how many people really seek you out. And, on the flip side (which of course I have to give you to prove my point), see how many people gravitate to the person sending out the good vibes. Actually pay attention to how being around that sort of person feels. Feels pretty good.

When I was a kid, my aunt Charlotte had an old sign on the wall of her New Hampshire ski house. Three simple words that said it all: *illegitimi non carborundum*. Don't let the bastards get you down. The same words hang in my house now. And I don't let 'em. And so far, so good.

It's Spring, Go On, Be Anal

Printed April 2013

Ah, spring.
We wait for it and we wait for it and we wait and we wait…still waiting…and then we wait a teeny bit longer…and then it comes. (You're sighing, I feel it.) And then it's all about crocuses and pastel shorts and beach stickers. I know, I feel you. And we all breathe and sigh and smile. My friend Jenny actually celebrates when we turn the clocks ahead. It's her favorite day of the year. You go, Jen!

But for me, spring has a much different meaning. For me, it's only partly about the flower bulbs and the shiny new grill brush. What really lights me up is actually the bastard child of spring. He's the one no one likes to talk about. You know him, he's the one we have to tolerate because he's a byproduct of the season, but the one we wish we could avoid because he makes a lot of people edgy and anxious.

I call that bastard child Spring-Cleaning. And I love him.

To me, spring means organizing and all that that implies. My friends are laughing now because they know that if a little girl got a pony for her birthday, she'd be as happy as I am when I get to switch out my winter clothes. But I can't help it. Just the idea of cleaning the slate and getting ducks in a row makes me happy. I guess it's kind of a Zen thing for me. My friend Liza is wetting her pants reading this because she knows cleaning is like my religion. Some people criss-cross applesauce under a weeping willow and chant "om"; some people get a hot rock massage. Me, I put on my nappy, old cutoff overalls, grab a handful of double-lined Glad bags, and I'm in my happy place.

In my little world, spring means filing, labeling, hanging, folding, purging, cleaning, and shredding (all right, now I'm getting flushed). I get giddy this time of year because spring affords me the almost God-given right to legitimately do something I'm inclined to do on just about any given day: clean, sort, and organize. Yeah, sure, I love a good spring mani-pedi just like the next girl, but give me a Brother P Touch Label Maker and some Joy Mangano Huggable Hangers and whoa, baby!

It's liberating tearing through underwear and sock drawers, filling bags to give to Goodwill or the Magic Hat Thrift Shop. But it's even more fulfilling to be able to go out and buy new underwear and new socks. That's the real fun.

Look, I know I might be a bit of a minority here, but I actually do get some kind of a bizarre high from switching out my riding boots for my wedges and Dr. Scholl's. We all have our weaknesses. I realize that most people switch over their winter/spring clothes and maybe pressure-wash their shingles under duress. I know it's not the norm to get this happy over something so tedious. But I just can't help myself.

So maybe you toss out a few old sweaters left over from the Dukakis days, Fantastik the vegetable crisper, and switch your knee-highs to your espadrilles. And that's all well and good. In fact, that's great. Whatever makes you happy. Look, I accept that I'm the extreme. I know who I am. But I can't help but think that you might be missing an opportunity here to dig deeper, to kick it up a notch, to transcend. You'd be amazed at what you can accomplish when you feel the weight of all your unwanted, unused crap just melt off you like those last annoying ten pounds of body weight that just won't come off. Cleaning does that. It's incredibly cathartic (and maybe almost some sort of a freaky diuretic, who knows). After all, purging yourself of ten pounds of unwanted clothes is almost as good as losing ten of your own pounds. Well almost.

Think of it this way: in much the same way that the world's spider population performs a great service to our ecosystem by keeping the insect population under control, we anal-retentive organizers and cleaners add value, too. I mean, every species has value, right? If it weren't for us purging all of our unwanted, obsolete stuff in your face, you wouldn't necessarily think you needed to get rid of anything. So we inspire you. Right?

Even if it's not your natural inclination, the least you could do is give it a try. Embrace your inner anal-retentive. You won't be sorry. And just think about how much room you'll have for all the new crap you'll be inclined to buy.

I mean, think about it, the universe wants us to purge regularly because the alternative is hoarding, and that's just pathological. You don't want to wind up on A&E, now do you?

I've never tried to hide who I am. I'm neat and I function better when my stuff is organized. Plain and simple. And I'm not embarrassed to say that because of this mild (well, moderate) form of anal-retentiveness, neither Dave nor I have misplaced our keys or a wallet more than twice in the last twenty years. A staggering statistic, I know. But true.

And there are others like me. I've met them. I've seen their post-spring- cleaning pantries, and they're stunning. Very *Sleeping with the Enemy*. Gives me chills. And their mudrooms give me a warm feeling inside when I see the individual baskets filled with shoes and the one next to them filled with scarves. Labeled. It really doesn't get better than that.

I think the superorganized tend to get a bad rap just because they represent a minority. And super-duper cleaning represents lots of extra work, I know. But the payoff is huge.

Bottom line is that people should live however they want to live. I don't judge anybody. Be neat. Be a slob. Dive head first into your spring-cleaning, or don't. Makes no difference to me. I could care less about anyone else's crap or whether or not I have to step over it when I visit you. If it's not in my little world, doesn't bother me a bit. I just function better when I'm organized. It's really that simple. And if being what might be considered anal-retentive makes me a freak, then I got my freak on fosho. Maybe you could get a little crazy this spring and get your freak on, too.

Shut Up and Get Moving!

Printed April 2013

This one's for you, ladies.

Guys, feel free to read on. This could be a rare, painless glimpse into the mind of your better half. And you're safe here—it'll be like looking through one-way surveillance glass on SVU; you can see us, but we can't see you.

So last week was spring-cleaning week, which means, historically speaking, that this week is Try-on-All-Your-Spring-and-Summer-Clothes-Hoping-They-Still-Fit Week. Not an officially recognized holiday, but still significant nonetheless. And a very touchy calendar marker for us girls.

Summer, she's a comin' like a runaway train. So like you, I'm trying like hell to get my groove on before it actually gets here. You know what I mean when I say groove, right, girls? It means bikini body and all that that implies. And for all you mature, seasoned ladies like me (and by that I mean over forty), it ain't easy. But it's a necessary evil, for sure.

Spring is always a dicey time of the year for us girls. It's when we see how hard we really fell off the exercise wagon over the winter. Did we just gently slide off the back and land softly on our slightly plumper rear end, or are we talking severe road rash and internal bleeding? Either way, it's painful. I know. I'm right there with you.

We're all dying to get into our skinny jeans, but none of us would be caught dead in them until we can safely button the top button and still exhale. About the only thing we've got going for us coming off of winter is the fact that our toes don't retain much water from season to season—and they look good right out of the gate after a decent mani-pedi. So you know what that means, girls; it just means we need to work from the bottom up. And we're women, are we not? No one's heartier than us. I mean, come on, if we can all manage labor and delivery, then losing a little winter weight is like a cakewalk. (Sorry, bad analogy under the circumstances.)

We all want the same things—good arms, good butt, good thigh gap—but what we all have to accept is that it's a helluva lot tougher to get and maintain than it was a decade or two ago. So right here and now I need you to just suck it up. Know it. Accept it. And let's move on. We aren't who we once were, but I think we can be better. Really. I think if we commit, we can just sidestep the whole aging thing altogether. I'm such a believer that age is a state of mind that I'm willing to call out aging right here publicly and say, "Screw you." That said, we can't just wallow in it anymore; we need to fight! We need to train harder and smarter and avoid looking aging in the eye no matter what it takes. So our metabolisms have started playing mean, nasty little tricks on us. So what. We can fight back. We can eat a tiny bit less; we can order the skinny latte; we can walk the dog instead of letting him out back on the runner. We have options. We always have options.

So this is what I need you to do. You need to get your game face on right now. Go on, dig it out of wherever you left it and put it on right now. It's probably behind your Nike Shox in the back of your cedar closet. We've got what, six weeks until Memorial Day? For God's sake, they can build a condo complex in six weeks. We've got a little weight to cut, and six weeks is like a lifetime. We just need to keep our eye on the prize, that's all..

All you really need is a little perspective. So here it is: *this is not going to happen overnight.* You're going to get pissy. You're going to get moody. (Sorry, guys.) And we're probably not going to be friends anymore because I'm making you do this. But it's OK, because once you're inspired and doing what I tell you to do, the weight *will* come off. Then you're gonna love me. Remember, there's strength in numbers and we're doing this together. So we're all in it to win it from this point on. Because, like anything, this is all just about attitude anyway. Attitude. Attitude. *Attitude.*

There's this saying I love (probably because it applies to just about anything): you are who you believe yourself to be. So if I brainwash you enough right now, you'll believe that you're a weight-loss machine, and you'll start dropping weight before you put down the paper.

Look, we're all in damage control mode right now. There isn't one of us out there who didn't get even a little soft this winter, myself included. It's just what happens when we live in a climate that offers season changes, which, in turn, offer bulky, concealing, forgiving clothing. But it's OK. Hibernation is over and it's go time.

What we all need to remember is that it takes almost exactly the same amount of time to put weight on as it takes to get it off. So we're skipping right over the pity party and getting straight to work. Consider this your kick in the ass. Sorry, but you needed it. Besides, that's what friends are for.

And guys, I think they're all set now. You're welcome.

A Little Healthy Perspective, Please

Printed April 2013

I like to keep a low profile. A little bit of an oxymoron, I know, given that I write an opinion column. But I really do keep most of my feelings to myself. It's safer that way. Plus, it's the number one survival rule for living in a peninsula town. If you don't want something coming back and biting you on the a**, keep your mouth shut. So aside from telling my thirteen-year-old daughter that cartilage piercings are a horrendous idea, I'm just not the proselytizing type. It's not my style.

But I'm compelled, certainly after the events of last week that affected us all, to ask that we take a healthy pause surrounding this business with our school committee that's been consuming so much of our attention lately.

Look, there are certain things that I've always believed are just too sacred, too personal to put out there for general consumption. These are the opinions I keep to myself. I call them the Big Three. They're like my own homegrown version of Bird, McHale, and Parish for Celtics fans. Only mine are Religion, Politics, and Jewelry. I try to never offer opinions about them unless I'm asked, and when I do, I'm usually pretty censored.

Only every so often do I make a rare exception. And it takes an epic event to move me enough to lay it all out there. So consider this one of my every-so-oftens. Today I'm talking. And I'm jumping right to the head of the line and talking town politics.

Let's just get something straight right off the line, though: I have no loyalties, no alliances, no favorites, no agenda, no backstory, and certainly no aspirations. What I have is nothing more than an opinion—that, and an enormous amount of respect for everyone in our system who has dedicated themselves to giving our kids every advantage available to be successful in their lives. And isn't that what it's all supposed to be about?

Truth be told, I have absolutely no interest in calling anyone out for anything specific. I think that's just counterproductive, not to mention a ridiculous waste of time, energy, and good newsprint.

Instead I'm going to be Switzerland. I'm staying neutral in the face of all the crazy. Because it is crazy. And considering the Swiss did it so well, I'm following their lead.

I'm not a politician, I'm not even particularly all that smart, but I think I have a reasonable amount of EQ (emotional quotient)—enough that I instinctively know that most of what's gone on within our school committee these past couple of months has gone way too far. It's honestly worse than the worst episode of *Dance Moms* I've ever seen. It's like I can't bring myself to watch it anymore, yet, at the same time, I can't seem to look away.

The sad thing is that it almost doesn't matter what's happened up to this point. It doesn't matter who's said what or who has the last word. Although, frankly, I'd love it to be mine. (Between you and me, I've always had this fantasy of being able to solve all the world's problems.) Through it all, a few people have made courageous, inspiring decisions, while others have deserved a time out more than either of my own kids ever have. Which is why, at this point, I think it should only be about one thing, and that's moving forward.

So I'm giving my opinion simply because what I think people really need right now is a voice of reason. Or, at the very least, a reasonable voice. (And maybe a light dope slap to the side of the head.)

I'm a rabid believer of owning it. And the lack of owning it I've been seeing lately could be the crux of our problem. In fact, I think, it's the root of most peoples' problems. Because when you really look close, most people just don't have the capacity (or the cojones) to take responsibility for their actions. I'm sure we can all agree that nothing good comes from finger-pointing and tit for tatting. Wasted time. It's only when people start owning their actions that most problems will generally resolve themselves.

So the fingers have all been pointed, and the tits have all been tatted. If you said it or did it, stand by it. And let's please move on. I think after this week we can all agree that we've all got much bigger fish to fry.

If there are capable people in our system who can elevate us to what we all hope to be—which is the common goal, is it not?—then it's time we let them do what we brought them here to do. Or rather, brought him here to do.

Yup, I just said that. I said him. And I'm owning it. Because I'm also a big believer that people cycle in and out of our lives at very specific times and for very specific reasons. We call that karma. And when karma speaks, you damn well better listen.

We've clearly veered off our course lately, but what does your GPS do when you choose to go left when it says go right? It recalculates the route and gets you there, in spite of the fact that you didn't listen the first time. So don't you think it's time we all listened to our GPS before we drive ourselves through the barrier at the end of the dead-end cliff?

Clearly we can't go back to where we've been, nor would we want to. But we can take with us what we've learned—the good, the bad, and the pathetic—and set a new course. Because if we navigate through life the way we're supposed to, we should be learning something as we go.

I'm a Header just like you, with an extremely vested interest in what goes on in the town I've lived in and loved my entire life. Sitting here typing, thinking about everything this little town means to me and now to my girls, I've got bona fide tears in my eyes and a lump in my throat. Like all true Headers, I bought all my penny candy at Tent's Corner and climbed the yellow cargo ropes in Mr. Piccard's Bell School gym class. I busted my chin open on the steps at St. Stephen's Nursery School and got my stitches to close it at the Mary

Alley Hospital. I've dived off every dock in the harbor and spent endless summers sidestepping seagull s--t on Children's Island. I've traveled through the Marblehead school system from beginning to end, graduating from both Tower School and Marblehead High. I've raised my children here, sat on PTO boards, been a room parent a dozen times over and, most recently, spent the last nine-plus years working in our school system. So, like you, I want to see my idyllic little harbor town rise from the ashes.

Why am I giving you my life story? For no other reason than to buy myself some respectable street cred. I need you to understand that I'm not a casual observer of what's gone on here. I'm vested, like you.

We need to think of this situation as if we're renovating one of our great historical landmarks that signifies who we are. We need to think of our school committee like it's Abbot Hall, rich in history and character but needing a little rehab to restore it to its former great self. And I think we all know that sometimes we just need to take it down to the studs to expose the flaws and see what we're really dealing with. Then we rebuild.

So here we are, down to the studs. Wires and framing exposed and everything out in the open. There's nothing left to do but rebuild with the common goal of moving forward. And personally, I think we've already found the right contractor for the job. Now let's just let him get busy and do the work.

(OK, so maybe not exactly Switzerland.)

Author's Note: It's worth mentioning here that this column was the byproduct of months of discontent within our town's school committee. Without getting into the gory details, the committee was irreparably divided over leadership or lack thereof. Lines were drawn, shots were fired, and small-town political careers were lost. The whole situation was a shame and uglier than any roadside accident I've ever seen, because a number of capable and loyal public servants were lost in the crossfire.

Grow Your Altruistic Footprint.

It's the New Black

Printed May 2013

So there's this scratch on my car. Nothing that's obvious to anyone but me and certainly not a big deal in the grand scheme of life. (Definitely not worth blowing my auto deductible.) Plus, I'm sure it was just someone's runaway Stop & Shop carriage anyway. Probably a little nudge sent by karma to get me back for something I did wrong in the eighties.

But as these innocent little things often do, it got me wondering. (I know, here I go again.)

Consider this: what kind of a world would it be if everyone put his or her shopping carts back in the little corral? Which, of course, in turn, leads me to wonder the even bigger question: what kind of world would it be if everyone who smoked tossed their cigarette butts in an actual trash can? Or, bigger still, what would Marshalls *really* be like if people rehung everything they knocked off the hanger while they browsed?

This is the stuff that consumes my thoughts at 2:00 a.m., when I'm wide awake and scribbling notes on my little notepad in the dark.

I know what you're thinking; I have way too much free time. That, or I need to up my Ambien script. But I really think, somewhere deep down, you've probably asked yourself these same philosophical questions, too. This is existentialism, baby. It's here that deep thinking starts.

I just can't help myself; I'm always thinking about ways we can all be better as people and, consequently, as a people. Because if you read my last column, you know that my ultimate reach goal in this life is to solve most of the world's bigger-ticket problems. Hunger. Poverty. Famine. Stupidity. (Hopefully before I retire so I can enjoy a perfect world while I'm still able to get around.)

Honestly, how many times have you wished, secretly, that people would just act for the benefit of other people once in a while? Because when you think about it, our little Earth could be a dramatically different place if everyone just thought of the other guy once every now and then.

Just imagine a world where each one of us returned our shopping carts to the corral. Think of how many innocent little BMW convertibles would ultimately be spared. Now I know this would have a negative impact on the auto insurance industry, domestic and foreign auto body shops, and the National Association of Independent Insurance Adjusters, but I can't solve everything on the first day. I'm just dealing with the outer layer of the onion here.

This not-taking-responsibility-for-our-own-stuff thing is reaching epic levels. I mean, let's look, even for a second, at how that applies to the whole carbon footprint movement. Think of what we could accomplish if everyone just did what the little hotel door-hanger sign says and reused our bath towel. Even once per vacation. My God! That alone would probably save President Obama's Land and Water Conservation Fund from expiring in 2015.

And what if everyone gave a thank-you wave when you stopped to let people cross the street? We're supposed to, you know. But few people actually do. I know. I'm watching you. Just that alone on a worldwide scale could have a direct impact on the world's happiness meter. (Which, by the way, is real. The government owns it. It just keeps it at Area 51 for deniability.) And what about saying thanks when someone holds the door for you? Or cleaning your dirty dishes off your café table at Panera before I sit down? Or, dare I say, tossing your McNuggets box in an actual trash can and not out your window on the Mass Pike. You're making my world look like crap.

Now these are all standard rules of behavior that should be hardwired into our psyche. Unfortunately, though, too many people are missing the gene. And that's when I think we as a culture get into collective trouble. That's when we see our landfills overflowing because people think nothing of littering. And that's when hotel laundry services strike because the demand for cottony fresh towels exceeds a reasonable limit. This stuff's real, people. And it needs to be addressed on both a grassroots and a global level.

Because it really is the little things. They're the ones that count. They're the most impactful. And when you add them all up, they could legitimately change the world. Both emotionally and physically.

Can you imagine if we took this whole notion of doing your part for yourself and others to the next level and asked everyone to do even one selfless thing every day? Holy hell! We'd be one exit away from nirvana. You know what I'm saying here, right? I'm talking about paying it forward. Wish I could take credit for the idea, but, sadly, I got trumped on that one. I'm a huge fan, though. Brilliant. Because, in the end, that's what I guess I'm really getting at. Just close your eyes and imagine a world where everyone was selfless (I'm thinking big here because this is my dream, so what the hell). We talk a lot about reducing our carbon footprints. Well, I think we ought to be just as conscious of growing our altruistic footprints. But in my version of this Brave New World, everything would also be pink. Sounds perfect, doesn't it?

This is 40: A Movie Review

Printed May 2013

Now I'd like to think that at this age and stage of the game (somewhere in my forties is all you need to know), I can consider myself many things. So let's go with the obvious first. At this moment I'm a columnist. I mean, duh. Less obvious, but way more important, I'm a mother and a wife. I'm also a landscaper; head chef; housecleaner; language arts, math, social studies, science, and foreign language tutor; anger management specialist; financial analyst; waste disposal technician; tech support rep; mediator; and amateur electrician. The range is broad. And I'm pretty sure that your business card reads a lot like mine.

What I am not, however, is a movie reviewer. (Didn't see that one coming, did you?) But since I'm a big fan of trying on lots of different hats, I think this is the perfect time and place to give movie reviewing a whirl. After all, I've got a captive audience just hanging on my every word (yeah, as if). Plus, the movie I'm talking about is totally relevant to what's on my mind anyway. One disclaimer though before I dive in: I'm a Joey to movie reviewing (otherwise known as a newbie), so I'm purposely setting the bar low here to ensure that failure is less painful. (For me, not you.)

So let me cut right to the chase…

If you haven't seen Judd Apatow's newest comedy, *This Is 40*, yet, see it. See it now. I mean stop doing whatever you're doing, find it, and watch it. All right, strike that. Finish reading the column, and then watch it. I need as much readership traction as I can get.

In a nutshell, *This Is 40* is a deliriously funny, albeit, at times, self-indulgent window into the midlife crisis of Pete and Debbie, a married couple turning forty and fighting it every step of the way.

It's your typical gratuitous comedy. Most of it is over-the-top, exaggerated humor (a lot like *Superbad*), but the relatability is so strong that it manages, in spite of its kookiness, to give you something to connect with on some level.

The film is such a hysterical and often painful rendering of what so many marriages evolve into once we hit our forties, that if you're anywhere within that fortysomething range, you'll relate to the movie somehow. If you've been married awhile, have any number of kids, and haven't fired off one cohesive sentence to your spouse in the last twelve months, then this is the movie for you.

A quick rundown of the plot: Instead of embracing their fortieth birthdays, Pete and Debbie are stalled in a midlife crisis with unruly kids, crushing debt, and an overhanging cloud of mutual annoyance. Pete's record label is failing, and Debbie just can't come to terms with her aging body. The entire movie is a comedy of errors. Which, when you think about it, is what most of our lives are like at that stage. Maybe not quite as far-fetched but close enough that we can identify with the sense that we're all constantly in motion, forever running on the same little wire hamster wheel but never really getting anywhere.

Like Pete and Debbie, most of us in this stage of life don't have three seconds to ourselves (not even in the bathroom, sadly). Many of us actually, secretly, relish opportunities to go to Market Basket and grocery shop alone, pathetic as that may be. (OK, maybe that's just me.) And every last one of us is desperate to keep The Flame burning white hot (winky, winky), but we're all just too damn tired to stoke it.

And that's the tie-in for me. That relatability. That's why I was so compelled to get all Gene Siskel on you. Because it occurred to me, while I was all but wetting my pants laughing during this movie, that so much of it was my life. And if so much of it was my life, then so much of it has to be yours, too.

So this time next week, Dave and I will trade in our crystal anniversary marker (that's fifteen for those of you, like me, who had no clue) for the big two-oh. We're trading up to the china anniversary. Yup, twenty years. Add it all up, and it amounts to two kids, two dogs, two Siamese fighting fish, two hamsters, one ball python (not sure what Dave was thinking with that one), one guinea pig, countless houses and jobs, at least as many milestones and crises, and one helluva beautiful ride.

It's called a labor of love for a reason, kind of like my yoga practice is called a practice—because it's never a finished work. And it's not supposed to be. Just like life is always a work in progress.

So when I watched this movie, blowing bits of popcorn out of my nose because I was laughing so hard, and I looked over at Dave, doubled over and laughing just as hard, I realized that this quirky little movie just summed up our entire life together. And we both felt it. And it was beautiful. We laughed at the good, we laughed at the bad, and we pissed our pants at the ridiculous. Because life is messy, life smells (mostly just after we run), life is harrowing, life is blissful, life is exhausting, life is infuriating, life is invigorating, and life is beautiful. And that's exactly the way it's supposed to be. And Apatow nails it in *This Is 40*.

Because it's at these big mile markers when we can pause for a second and glance back at how far we've come, and we can say "I love you" and still mean it; then we know we've got something real.

So, I love you, babe. It's been one helluva ride.

(Now you can go watch the movie. Go on, go.)

This Year's Memorial Day was an Exercise in 'Nimbility'

Printed May 2013

So I know what you're thinking...Mother Nature can be a nasty bitch. I mean, who does she think she is, sabotaging Memorial Day weekend by shutting off the heat and cranking up the wind and the rain? I think she should have more consideration than that, don't you?

I mean, honestly, no one's more hyperaware of what we go through all winter than her, right? She's got club seats to watch us tough it out all winter, through the nor'easters and the blizzards and the black ice on nothing more than the promise that spring will be exactly where it's supposed to be at exactly the time that's printed on the calendar. She knows that we make our plans, we confirm our reservations, we send out our invitations all according to the dates that she sets. She's conditioned us to believe that winter is only temporary. I mean, hell, we've got calendars printed all over the world with dates that are supposed to be credible. Jeez. And she even sends us signs to confirm it, too. Around mid-April everything starts exploding around us—trees start to bud, lawns start to thicken, and we see Memorial Day in the distance like the finish line tape in our annual Winter Marathon.

Unfortunately, though, this year Mother Nature got feisty and gave us a reminder that she's still the one calling the ball. Maybe she was feeling fickle. Girls get fickle. Maybe she was feeling moody.

Girls get moody. Or maybe she was just feeling bitchy. God knows girls get bitchy. Who knows? I just know it was very inconsiderate of her. I mean all those poolside barbecues and spring weddings and yard sales and outdoor events that are predicated on warm weather and bluebird skies had to be scrapped. It's a disappointment, I know. She pulled the same thing on me twenty years ago on my wedding day. It was supposed to be seventy-five and sunny, with two-mile-an-hour winds and just the right number of birds chirping in the trees. But she laughed at me that day, and she pulled the same crap she pulled last weekend. She got all righteous and said, "Uh-uh, girl-friend, not today." But we adapted. We were nimble. We had to be. We had no choice. So we regrouped and headed indoors. And it was perfect, in spite of her.

I know it seemed like this year was just another one of Mother Nature's nasty little jokes, tossing a windy, cold Memorial Day week-end at us for no good reason. But I've gotta tell you, since my wed-ding weekend two decades ago, I've learned that she's only one player on Team Universe. She doesn't have all the power. She's just one of many. There's Father Time, the Grim Reaper, the Sandman, Cupid. They're all just players, no different than Mother Nature. They're all part of a bigger team, and they don't get to call the shots. I learned that we, as freethinking human beings, are equipped with the ability to be nimble and react to our environment. We're all actu-ally designed with the built-in capacity to adapt to our surroundings. It's called human biological adaptability. Yup, it's real. (I'm not smart enough to make this stuff up.). We actually have the power to over-ride the universe using the power of "nimbility." (It's on Wiktionary, so there's a fifty-fifty chance that it's a real word. But it was exactly the word I was looking for.)

Look, there's a huge part of me that would've loved to have spent the weekend parked in a lounge chair at my friend Kim's pool, slathered in Coppertone, with a Red Stripe in hand and a burger balanced on my knee, but I'm not too disappointed that I actually spent most of the weekend inside, bundled up in yoga pants, flip-ping between old episodes of *Chopped* and CNN.

I've learned to think of these little curveballs that Mother Nature sends as her version of a bye. And we all know that we need a bye every once in a while. Why do you think they're written into every professional sport team's calendar? Because they're essential to peak performance. They're like a hard reset. They're permission to do nothing, entitlement to be lazy. And we need that.

'Cause let's face it, we're all in constant motion. For me, if I'm not working, I'm driving one of my kids somewhere. If I'm not driving one of my kids somewhere, I'm driving someone else's kids somewhere. If I'm not chauffeuring someone, I'm running or biking or hiking or kayaking or golfing. Bottom line: if the sun is out, I'm inclined to be in it.

I don't stop very often, mostly because I believe in seizing the day. And because I'm almost always disposed to be out doing something, I rarely sit in one place long enough to make a mark in the cushion. Example: I'm still reading the same book I started in January, if that's any indicator. I know, I'm pathetic. But my constant motion, and the fatigue that it produces, has taught me to appreciate these byes that the Universe throws my way. I've learned that rainy days are the Universe's way of saying it's OK to downshift. And I've learned to love that. Because for all the dumb things that the Universe does, like create earthquakes and floods and other ridiculous types of natural disasters, rainy, crappy days that force a hard stop are its way of giving back.

So while my pale little legs are wishing they'd had some good pool time this weekend, my relaxed mind and body are grateful that Mother N. threw me a bye. Thanks, girl. Guess you're not the total "biatch" I thought you were.

Don't Hate the Technology, Hate the User

Printed June 2013

So what's the best way to say this without sounding like an ass? I guess ripping the Band-Aid right off is probably the way to go.

I. Hate. Mobile. Technology.

OK, I know, that was harsh. And slightly hypocritical. I'm sorry. I guess what I really mean is that I love it, but I hate it at the same time. It's a lot like how I feel about Shaun T, the crazy fitness trainer who leads my *Insanity* workouts. I love him for what he does for me, but I hate him for how he does it.

Look, I have a husband who works in mobility, so I've got all kinds of mobile technology raining down on me like the monsoons in Asia. It's unrelenting. And while I don't want to sound ungrateful for all these neat little toys, the irony is that if I had my way, I'd still be using a rotary phone and a Marblehead Savings Bank pocket calendar to manage my life. I'm just a simple girl who likes simple things. Sadly, though, those days of hearing an actual busy signal are gone, and I've been pushed into the smartphone pool headfirst. And while I will admit that after some soaking I did adjust to the water quite nicely, I still have a lot of nostalgia for the good ol' days, when the toughest thing about making a phone call was getting the accordion door on the payphone booth to stay shut.

I really do get all the benefits of having so much functionality packed neatly into my back pocket at all times. I do. It's almost like having an RV without the wheels—I've always got everything I need to sustain me right there whenever I need it, with the exception of running water and the ability to fix myself a ham sandwich. The main thing, I guess, I struggle with is the intrusion factor of it all. And for me, that's an obstacle I'm not sure I'll ever get over. Because they're everywhere. All the time.

Our phones have become like another appendage, almost like another child even, when you think about it. We take them with us everywhere, we try to find the cutest ways to dress them up, we're so proud of what they can do, we feel hollow and unsettled whenever we have to leave them behind, and we focus most of our energy on ensuring their safety and well-being. I mean God forbid it falls, right?

Think about it, we wake up and we check our phone. We step away from our desk for *any* length of time (and I'm talking even seconds); we check our phone. We need to check our calendar; we reach for our phone. We want to call someone; where's my cell? We need to snap a photo (and then immediately upload it to Instagram); camera's in the phone. We need to look up the word "quixotic"; we use the Dictionary.com app…on our phone. That sense of instantaneous connectivity has been embedded in us, embedded in our kids. But I'm not so sure that's such a great thing.

Because if you look closely, it looks an awful lot like smartphones are photo bombing all of our lives a little more every day. They're part of everything now. And we're moving further and further away from doing the simple things that used to give us all so much pleasure. Things like talking. Things like listening. Things like waiting, patiently.

People have become paranoid that they're missing something if they're not connected. But the truth is, they're missing things just by *being* so connected. Seems like once smartphone technology really went mainstream, so did everyone's new compulsion to constantly check their phone every four seconds for that rogue post that snuck in under the radar. And I'm guilty of it. For sure. And it makes me crazy because I hate feeling like this dopey, little plastic box in my pocket has that much control over me. Because I really don't want it to. But it's especially powerful when you have kids because having a cell phone, in a lot of ways, is like having an extralong umbilical cord.

So when that phone vibrates, you bet I'm all over it like white on rice to make sure they can reach me when they need me.

Dave and I have this ongoing debate about the intrusiveness of mobile technology. He sees only virtues and benefits. He thinks technology makes us better, faster, and more efficient. (He also loved Star Trek and all that when he was a kid, so it's life imitating art for him.) And while I can't deny any of those obvious benefits, my secret fantasy is really to drop every device in my house into a steel box and bury it in the Badlands. But that comes from my simple opinion that too much of a good thing almost always becomes a bad thing.

My fear is that we're becoming more and more reliant on these things every day and less and less capable of living without them. It's like when my kids are trying to reach a friend to make plans and their friend doesn't respond to their text right away. That stops them cold. They truly don't know how to react. And when I suggest picking up the phone and just calling, I get the "pfffffft," and then they slam their bedroom door. And I know that that's because I grew up lying upside down against my bedroom door talking to my friends on the phone. Real voices. Real conversations. But that was my generation, not theirs.

So while I get why we're moving in the direction we're moving, I just don't want to see us devolve any more than we already have. Remember, retro is in for a reason. Because deep down, we all have a fondness for the good old days. So do me a favor. The next time you grab your cell to text me, gimme a call instead, for old time's sake. I promise I'll answer.

No More Driving Miss Daisy

Printed June 2013

So I'm standing at the edge of a precipice. The same one my mother stood at before me. It's so high I'm not sure I can make out the bottom. My toes are hanging off the edge, and little rocks are starting to break away and fall under my feet. It's a long way down. A long way. My heart is pounding in my chest, like it does when you're confronting someone about something upsetting and you're trying to keep yourself calm. I can hear the beating in my head. It's so loud. I keep forgetting to breathe.

I know I have to jump. I have no choice. I know it's going to change everything. I know the landing might be ugly, but I have to move forward. I know I do. It's the only direction I can go. I'm exhilarated and petrified at the same time. Knowing that millions have gone before me and survived isn't giving me as much comfort as I thought it would. But I need to stay positive.

I force myself to lean forward. Momentum is taking over now. The wheels are in motion. It's time. I draw in one last deep breath. I shut my eyes and step forward. Then I hear it. The voice is faint. I hear it again. It's louder now. "May I help you?" I look up, startled. "I said, may I help you?" I nod. I must look confused. Bewildered, maybe. I ask where I should go from here. The woman points to a sign over her shoulder. I read it quickly, but my mind is racing so it's hard to focus. I finally make out the words: Learner's Permit Test Registration. I'm airborne now. I'm in free fall.

All right, so maybe I took a little bit more creative license here than I needed to. But when I've imagined what it's going to feel like later this afternoon at the DMV when I take Riley for the real test, that's pretty much how it was playing out in my mind.

As parents, we're constantly hopping from stage to stage with our kids. We breeze right through the little ones, like dropping their spoon every time we turn around or cruising from couch to chair to table. And we knuckle down and dig in for the more challenging ones like learning to ride a bike or how to nicely ask the boy next to you to borrow his pencil sharpener instead of punching him in the face and grabbing it. Clearly some phases are more challenging than others. There are those that require constant helicopter parenting, like biting, spitting, and hair pulling, while others are way less complicated like reminding them to zip up their fly before leaving the house. All of them, though, take a certain measure of TLC. And thankfully for us, the range is vast so we usually have time to inhale.

I've said it before, but I'm saying it again…this parenting thing we do is a labor of love, for sure. I mean our mettle is constantly being tested with all the different hoops we have to jump through, and "nimble" is usually the word of the day. Of all the phases and stages, though, this driving stage is a real curveball, probably because it's hard to know how to feel about it.

OK, so my days of driving Miss Daisy are almost over. On the one hand, I'm thrilled that I won't have to pack a bag lunch and my book and live out of my car as much anymore during the week, driving my kids everywhere and back fifty times a day. Although, between you and me, I love those drives, especially the ones when the kids start talking and forget that I'm there. That's how I get all my insider information. But on the other hand, I'll have plenty of time to take that Science of Superheroes class through the University of California at Irvine that's been on my list. There's always an upside.

Now look, I'm supremely confident that Riley will be a good driver. (God, I hope you're listening. Please be listening.) We've taken her to the parking lot behind the temple to practice at least a half dozen times so far, and she's doing great. Granted, that's a wide-open space with no obstacles and an unlimited turning radius, but you've gotta start somewhere, right? Plus, she's secretly been driving the golf cart at Kelly Greens since she was fourteen. And now that we've all but forgotten the time she two-wheeled the cart around the thirteenth hole, it's all good. Everyone deserves a do-over, right?

I wish I could say I had some stellar advice for my chicklet as I send her out into the wild, but I don't. Sorry. The reality is, it's a different world now than it was when they put my permit in my hot little sixteen-year-old hands. More distractions. More cars on the road. More to worry about. Frankly, I'm not even sure I should still be on the road considering how much driving has changed. But I suppose, like everything, it's all relative to the world they're growing up in. Their brains have somehow learned to accept all the chaos around them. And I guess we should be grateful that their generation has evolved to this higher state of being.

So I guess the only thing for me to do is say a Hail Mary and cross my fingers. Tight. Oh, wait. Damn. I'm a Jew. So no can do. Hail Marys, I've heard, are nontransferable. No exceptions. Oh hell.

Well, under the circumstance, I guess I need to punt. So here goes. Keep 'em at ten o'clock and two o'clock, babe. Ten and two. And remember, the AAA card is in the glove box. Go get 'em, champ.

To Parents with Teenage Kids: Duck and Cover!

Printed July 2013

I distinctly remember being a kid once. I do. I mean there are hundreds of pictures and stories proving that I was one. So it definitely happened. My mom confirms it. But the crazy thing is, my kids don't buy it. They refuse to see me as anything but their mom. And I'm so much more than that, but there's just some little mechanism in the kid brain than inhibits that kind of information from being processed and absorbed. I'm "Mom" and that's it. It's like the second I gave birth I became a one-hit wonder.

It kills me that my being their mother automatically downgrades my cool rating to almost zero just by default. And that's just because to our kids, once we have that parent moniker, we're no longer a credible resource. Our past life just calcifies right there in front of our eyes and blows away like a loose pile of soot. And I know it's not just me. It's all of us, every last one of us. It's like we're condemned to be viewed only one way by our kids and never as the total package that we really are. And. That. Makes. Me. Crazy.

I'm not quite sure that I understand why our children can't view us like everyone else in the general population does. I mean, I look like other moms. I sound like other moms. So why then, when I say the same things that other moms say, does it always provoke the same superloud sigh, followed by a door slamming? Tell me, please.

Despite my constantly reminding them that there's probably very little that either of them will ever do that I haven't done, they still think I have no idea what the hell I'm talking about.

I mean, I remember getting punished (although rarely, because I was mostly awesome). I also remember making bad choices (also rarely, because of my awesomeness). I listened to music too loud and refused to wear sunscreen. I'm positive I was a general pain in the ass at least a small percentage of the time. (OK, fine, maybe it was like sixty-forty.) I remember thinking I knew absolutely everything about everything. I remember liking boys (probably too many boys, now that I think of it). I went to prom. I learned to drive. I stressed over grades. I assumed I could eat anything and metabolize it all away (I know, right!). I was bullied. I unconditionally bought in to the unspoken social hierarchy that existed within my school and accepted the fact that I was pretty much a bottom-feeder. I shared secrets. I kept secrets. I stalked boys. I just said no, about a million times. I felt anxious. I felt judged. I felt invincible. I felt scared. I felt the thrill of my first kiss, my first job, my first car. And I felt the pain of my first rejection, my first bombed interview, and my first pet dying. I ran the gamut. All of us did.

Clearly I've had sex at least twice, so I feel like I can speak to that when it comes up. But as far as my girls are concerned, Dave and I are asexual.

Most of the time, though, my kids treat me like I have absolutely no idea what the hell they're going through on a daily basis. And I'm not sure if that's more sad or funny.

And I love it when someone else gives them the exact same advice that I give them, and they treat it like it's the gospel. But when I say it, I just get "Mom! You! Have! No! Idea!" I get that a lot.

Now don't misunderstand me, I feel extremely lucky that my two kids were the ones who swam their little guts out up that fallopian tube. I'm blessed, I really am. They're both beautiful people, and I'm beyond lucky that they're mine. I just wish our kids could realize, when they're still kids, that we're so much more than just the nags who bitch at them to pick up all their crap off the floor and hang up their friggin' bathrobe. I mean, that's what the hook is for!

I feel like we should all be celebrated as parents, not avoided in public places and shunned because we have no rhythm or have no business getting a belly ring at age forty-four. Can't that just be cool on me like it would be on anyone else?

I can't help but feel that I have some degree of wisdom to impart, yet my kids instantly, and without any basis, discredit 99.7 percent of the advice or suggestions I give them purely because it was my womb they came out of.

Out in the real world, people seem to like my groove when I get it on. People actually listen to me and even, on rare occasions, ask my advice.

I don't get how we have no credibility with the very same little people we bring into the world.

I just don't get it. I've lived. I've screwed up. I have stories and wisdom. I've got game. But under my own roof, I'm no better than Rodney Dangerfield. I get no respect.

Look, I know my kids love me. But I want them to want me to start dancing in the middle of Forever 21 when the Muzak gets my groove on. I want them to want me to hang out in the basement when they're making up code names for the boys they like. I want them to hang on my every word and obey my every command.

Yeah, I know, I'm an idiot. Not gonna happen. And I'm pretty sure, now that I'm really thinking it through, that every generation faces the same issue.

Fortunately our kids get it eventually. Unfortunately for us, though, they don't usually get it until they have their own kids. At which point the old what-goes-around-comes-around kicks in and our justice is served piping hot with a cocktail on the side. That's when they'll see me for all that I really am. So until then, I guess I'll just duck and cover and ride the wave until it breaks. And you might consider doing the same.

Where have all the Good People Gone?

Printed July 2013

You know me, I'm an optimist. It's just how I'm wired. I always see the cup as half full. Usually spilling over. Can't help it. Life just doesn't make sense to me any other way. My natural inclination is to see the positive in people and in situations. Anything less seems silly. But sometimes that's not possible. Not even for me. Sometimes I see something that shakes my faith a little. Something that just makes me hang my head down low and shake it back and forth. Back and forth. And wonder how people can be so unaffected and cold to the people and things around them.

Most stuff I can just slough off, especially when it doesn't affect me directly. Like when I see someone chuck a Wendy's bag out a car window on the Pike. It stings for a second and then I refocus and I'm over it. Or when the dink in the Market Basket parking lot boxes out the ninety-three-year-old woman in the Lincoln Town Car to snag her spot. Dave usually sees me tense up as if I'm gonna get out of the car and throw down. Then he gives me the look he's given me since the eighties, the one that says, "Chill, babe. Karma will get him in the end. Let it go." And he's right.

But the things I can't let go of are the things people do that just defy even basic, fundamental core value systems. Values like kindness. I mean, in terms of human circuitry, kindness should be one of the lead wires, right?

Let me frame something for you, and you tell me. What would you do if you were driving down Humphrey Street one afternoon and you saw two high-school-age girls on the side of the road, one clearly injured, probably from a fall while she was running, and the other consoling her? Would it make you pause? Would you be compelled to stop and make sure they were all right? Would you offer your cell so they could call for someone? Or would you look the other way and keep driving?

I'll never know how you're answering, but believe me when I say I hope you weren't one of the cars who drove by my daughter and her bloodied friend as they stood on the side of the road a few weeks ago. Because it would make me extremely sad, and I'm afraid we couldn't be friends anymore. So I'm giving you the benefit of the doubt.

Sadly, my daughter (normally I'd use her name, but she's sixteen and hates it when I mention her name in my columns, so let's call her Norma) and her friend were out for an afternoon run when a metal ring on the side of the road snagged her friend's foot (let's call her friend Jean...get it, Norma Jean.) Jean went down hard. So hard that she looked a lot like a biker who dumped her Harley and got a bad case of road rash. Her knees, elbows, and palms looked like coleslaw, shredded and nasty. She looked like she'd barely made it out of a steel cage match on the WWF, blood dripping down both legs and clearly shaken. She was a mess. Poor kid. Now keep in mind, I didn't see her until most of the blood on her torn-up knees had already coagulated. Why? Because they were stuck on the side of the road in the one and only spot in the entire town where cell coverage doesn't exist. It's a mini-Bermuda Triangle, a freak of cellular nature. Great that they had a phone with them, but useless.

It's unclear exactly how long they were on the side of the road hitting redial. All I know is that by the time the cell gods granted them mercy and allowed their call to ring through to me, the blood on Jean's knees had completely clotted. Bottom line: they were there for a while.

When the call finally came through, this is how it sounded on my end: "Hey, Mom, uh, look, it's not life threatening or anything, but Jean took a pretty bad fall and she's pretty banged up. She can't run.

Can you come get us?" Not the worst call a parent can get, but still enough to make your heart bang a little louder in your chest, for sure.

I first spotted the trail of blood streaming down Jean's legs at about a hundred yards away; that's how noticeable it was. There was no mistaking that she had taken a digger. So why then do you suppose no one stopped to check on these kids all that time they were standing by the side of the road? You know, bleeding.

What! The! Hell?! I mean why, or rather how, did not one car stop? I really hope it's as baffling to you as it is to me. Could it have been that they looked too shady and threatening in their Nike Frees and reversible sports bras? Did it look like a setup? Like an elaborately contrived carjacking scheme? I mean, really?

I ask you: Where have all the good people gone? I could've sworn they were out there. I know so many of them.

So, of course, this all leads me to ask: Why isn't the world inundated with random acts of kindness? Why? Why are those acts the exceptions and not the norm? I know these pay-it-forward folks are out there. And I also believe that there are way more good people out there than bad. Problem is, people are still forgetting how to step forward and put themselves out there. Traits like kindness and empathy and advocacy that human beings should automatically be hardwired with, in spite of any other character flaws, are all qualities that I think the human framework is supposed to come with right off the shelf. No?

So put yourself in my place (which is something I don't think we all do enough of) and imagine it was your child bleeding on the side of the road. Would you hope that I would stop for them? I think we both know the answer. Now tuck that feeling somewhere in the back of your mind, and the next time you see someone who could use a hand, offer it. Please. Oh, and thanks in advance.

Kindness: It's a Game Changer

Printed July 2013

D o your kids ever cringe when you do certain things? Yeah, OK, I know, that was a rhetorical and relatively dumb question. Of course they do. Just like mine.

There are the obvious things that set them off like singing *any* music whatsoever in both public and private places. It's hard to say what irritates them more, me singing the music from my generation or when I get jiggy and try to sing theirs. Either way, it's always a major strike against me. There's also car, elevator, or mall dancing. That's practically like a mortal sin as a parent, punishable by evil and penetrating stares, usually followed by door slamming. Then there's my personal favorite, the, "I love you, baby, have the *best day ever*" out the window at school drop-off. Priceless at the high school. Or the two-fingered whistle on the sidelines at the home cross-country meets. All these things produce instant mortification. I know it and you know it and yet none of us can seem to help ourselves. It's like as soon as we have our own kids, our brains are scrubbed clean of any memory of how badly our parents embarrassed us, and we do the exact same thing to our kids. Like childbirth and why we keep going back for more. Once the initial pain and suffering of the delivery is over, we forget the agony, and all we remember is the happy, squishy baby.

But there is *one thing* I do in public that both my girls support. In fact, over the years, they've both actually started reminding me to do it. I have this habit of calling restaurant managers over to our

Lisa Sugarman

table during a meal to compliment our server if he or she is doing a really good job. I've been doing it since they were little, and they absolutely love it. In fact, one of them will usually whisper to me to do it during the meal if the server is particularly stellar. Cracks me up. I know it may not sound like much, but when you're there in person, seeing people's reaction to getting a compliment when they're sure they're about to get hosed is priceless. And I'm not sure what my kids like more, the fact that we're giving someone kudos for a job well done or the relief of the manager when they learn that what we have to say is good.

Because God knows that the restaurant managers I've spoken to over the years (and there have been many) all overwhelmingly say that they rarely, if ever, hear anything positive from their customers. And that's sad. But, unfortunately, the scales are almost always tipped way over on the complaint side. And what message does that send? Negativity, as far as I'm concerned. And negativity, I believe, is a completely hollow and useless emotion. It gets you nothing and nowhere. And it makes you look really, really bad.

Think about it, what do you tend to hear more from people, compliments or complaints? Complaints. Hands down. I mean, think about how often you've been out to dinner and you've seen someone flip a nutty on a server over a piece of meat that comes out too pink. Or an order that took a little too long. Or a dish that was cold. How many times have any of us been too quick to snap out a complaint when something isn't just right? And how ugly does that complainer look to you? Especially someone who really goes at it, ripping someone else to shreds. It's upsetting. And it's embarrassing.

So at the end of the day, what do our complaints really get us? A nasty reputation? Yup. Someone else's spit in our entrée? Absolutely. Possibly a foot in the ass? Maybe.

I mean, as a patron you're entitled to expect a good dining experience, and you're even encouraged to be vocal if you're not getting what you ordered. Because it *is* your money, after all. But herein lies the problem with the way most people are vocal—it's not about *what* you say as much as *how* you say it. Even if the food you're served is

94

terrible and the service is the suckiest you've ever had, there's a way to communicate this that won't make you look like an a-hole and will still get your point across. There's no need to tear someone down.

Because you and I know that this tendency people have to complain isn't just relegated to the restaurant world. It's everywhere. Like everywhere. And it bums me out. We see it all the time. People get pinpoint focused in the moment and act on raw impulse. And for a lot of people, their impulse is to find fault and complain before they stop and remember that there's a real, live person on the other end of that complaint. They attack the person and not the problem. And they forget that a little sensitivity and kindness goes a long, long way.

Just think about the last time someone gave you an unsolicited compliment. Think about how juicy and delicious it was. Think about how much you wanted to savor it because of how good it felt. How satisfying.

That's what compliments do. They bring out the best in people. They're a game changer.

So the next time you're out and someone goes above and beyond for you, go above and beyond for them. Play this goofy little game we play and see where it gets you. But be careful, you may just get addicted. Start slow and then build.

Bucket List: Get One!

Printed August 2013

Now I'm not trying to be an ass here; I'm just stating a fact. So don't be mad. But as of today, we've more or less hit the half-way point of our little summerfest, it being August and all.

I know, that hurt. I'm sorry.

And I know it's just as painful to hear it from me, as it is to see it up close when you walk down the back-to-school aisle in Target. (That, by the way, has been there since the fifth of July.) We have to face it at some point. But what we do with the knowledge of that painful truth is an entirely different story.

It's a devastating reality that all summers will eventually end, but the way I see it, sometimes a good ol' come to Jesus is a good thing. Sometimes forcing us to look something we're afraid of straight in the eye takes away the fear or the hatred or the anger and compels us to take control and act. Otherwise, we just sit around wallowing in the fact that something good will eventually end, and we forget about how much time we actually have left and how much we can still accomplish.

I won't lie, when I tore the month of July off my calendar this morning and exposed the second half of the summer, it got me a little edgy. I'll admit it. And if it got me edgy, then I'm sure on some level it's got you feeling a little uneasy, too. But I'm not giving in to the feeling that it's winding down. I just won't. Instead I've decided to grab summer by the crotch and hang on until it falls down to its knees and agrees to slow the hell down.

Lisa Sugarman

Then I'm going to force myself to stay in the moment and be completely present in this second half of summer and enjoy it every bit as much as I did the first half.

So I've decided to dig my summertime bucket list out of my nightstand and get serious. And while I have only a vague memory of what's on it, because I wrote it during one of our twenty-seven snow days this past winter, I'm going to tick through everything I've managed to do so far. Then I'm committing all the time we have left to finishing the rest, or coming pretty damn close. And whether I check off everything or not isn't the point. That doesn't matter. What matters is that I do my best to fulfill my own expectations.

And I think you should do the same. It'll be good for you. Plus, it's something we can do together. And it's always better to do something with a buddy.

You've got your list, right? Please tell me you have your list. Maybe it's just some scribbles on a cocktail napkin or a Post-it Note or the back of your Marshalls receipt. (Because those absolutely count.) But you've gotta have something tangible. Everyone needs something tangible.

And don't tell me your list is in your head because that, in fact, does not count. Mental lists are totally unreliable and will not be accepted. They get jumbled and confused and mixed with other lists when they're left floating around in your head.

And they're also incredibly susceptible to being erased from your memory when other more timely lists take their place, such as which kid you have to pick up at which friend's house on which day at what time and in what order.

And if you don't believe me that it's important to have real, clearly defined, written goals, then just pick up any self-improvement book and you'll see that having a to-do list is always somewhere in the first chapter. Guaranteed.

Plus, I think it's just plain necessary to reach outside your sweet spot and put things on your list that are at least a little out of your ordinary range. Otherwise, what's the point?

My girl Eleanor Roosevelt once said, "The purpose of life, after all, is to live it, to taste experience to the utmost, to reach out eagerly and without fear for newer and richer experiences." And if a shy, lonely city girl like Eleanor could figure that out at the turn of the century, then damn, we should all be aiming for the moon, considering everything that's out there for us to take advantage of.

So consider this your wake-up call for the rest of the summer. Imagine I'm holding the calendar right up to your face and forcing you to see how much time we've got left so you'll make the most of it. I know, it's tough love, but I don't want to see you blow five perfectly good weeks and not have something meaningful to show for it.

And remember, no one can judge what's on your list. That's the beauty of the bucket list. It's yours. And as long as it includes something exciting and meaningful and out of the ordinary for you, then it's perfect. Like if you're the type who never plants yourself in a lounge chair and relaxes by the beach, then that needs to be on your list. Or if you're a recreational runner who wants to kick it up a notch, then you should have a road race on your list. Get what I'm saying?

Just promise me you'll look deep and really flesh out the things that have been swimming around in your head. And then you'll write them down. And then you'll actually do some of them while you have the time. Because we do still have plenty of time, in spite of what the Old Navy back-to-school commercials have to say.

Seventeen Again

Printed August 2013

So here I am, in the car, on my way home from our first college tour. The University of Vermont. And to be honest, I'm not exactly sure if the motion sickness I'm feeling right now is because I'm typing while Dave's driving or because we're on our way home from our first college tour. Too tough to call. We've still got a couple of years left to let the reality of college ferment before it's palatable, but it was definitely a big moment.

Actually, I'm really pretty OK with the idea right now, mainly because Riley is so OK with it. Thank God for that whole cycle-of-life thing. I'm grateful for that little hidden layer of protection woven into all of us that buffers us just enough from the sadness of letting our kids go. Sort of like the fire-retardant suits firefighters wear that allow them to tolerate the heat of a barn burner without actually getting burned. They still feel the heat but without too much injury. Right now, to me, college is like that.

Either way, the whole trip got me thinking. Reminiscing, really. Remembering back to the perspective I had when I was seventeen and thinking about the perspective I have now. And lemme tell you, looking back now at where I came from then, I realize just how radically different those perspectives are just by virtue of nothing more than age and wisdom.

Think about it, even if you were a pretty grounded college freshman, which, knowing you, I'm sure you were, it wasn't like you never screwed up. It's inevitable. Happens to the best of us. You skipped class. You went to keggers. You went to your Introduction to Theory of Literature lecture with dark Wayfarers on and a really pounding headache and a queasy stomach. You did. We both know you did.

So haven't you ever wished you could go back and do it again? Knowing what you know now. Can you just imagine? Looking back, I think I really could've had a good shot at a Mensa membership if I retained even half of what I was exposed to when I was in college. And I actually tried in school. Like really tried and really put myself out there. But even in spite of that, looking back as an adult and a mom, I know I could've put myself out there even more than I did. I just know there's plenty I let fall through the cracks just because, at seventeen, what the hell did I know? Right?

And now that the whole college process is dangling a few inches out in front of me again, like Swifty the dog track rabbit, I'm kind of wishing there was a way I could go back again. But this time it would be as me now, not me then. And wouldn't that be something? Because this time I'd be totally present in the moment instead of just flitting from party to party. Uh, er, I mean moment to moment. (Sorry, Mom.) This time I'd suck it dry. I'd get everything I could out of it. And, I'm pretty confident, without even so much as a keg stand.

Because what most of us inherently lacked the first time around, even in spite of how ready for college we were, was appreciation. And it's only with age that we acquire wisdom, and it's only with wisdom do we learn appreciation. And these qualities are learned, believe me. They don't come standard. They take decades of life experience to develop before they're fully refined. And even then we're not perfect. That's why I think adults should automatically get a midlife do-over period that's automatically built into our late adulthood. Because, let's be honest, there probably isn't one of us who wouldn't want to pack our bags and do it all over again knowing what we know now. We could kill it if we went back and used all the life experience we've learned up to now.

And, of course, since this is my fictitious and totally impossible little brainchild, I think the whole thing should be government subsidized, maybe worked into Social Security somehow. I'll need more time to work out the higher-level details. So for now, let's just call it the Mature-Adult Higher Education Program, which would allow people to take advantage of all the wisdom and perspective they've acquired in their adult life and use it to go back and get more out of college than they did the first time. Then, just imagine how productive we'd be when we returned to our lives to finish out our careers?

Maybe the program is a year, maybe two. I picture the curriculum as a condensed version of the four-year programs most of us took as undergrads. The only difference being that it could be accelerated because most of us wouldn't be partying or sleeping in or missing classes. And since the majority of us have pretty decent executive functioning by now, we should be able to stay focused and actually retain what we're learning in that shorter time frame. Hell, maybe we could even get "life credits" and earn ourselves another degree. It could be like a BA in life.

And since we'd be doing this at a point in our lives when our kids are either in college or just out of school, we'd be totally unencumbered by distractions. Because remember, part of my plan is that the government pays our tuition *and* our employers give us an automatic sabbatical from our jobs (fully paid, of course).

I don't know where all this is going. I just know that this is the kind of thing my mind thinks about on five-hundred-mile road trips. Sorry.

Let's just say this, applications for the fall of 2014 are now being accepted. I figure it shouldn't take more than a year to sell the US Department of Education on the idea. You think? So get your Trapper Keepers out, 'cause who says you can never go back?!

When I Come Back, I'm Coming as a Dog

Printed August 2013

So this is going to come at you from a little left of center, but it's a monsoon out there this morning, and the worn-out leather couch at Starbucks has swallowed me whole. So I'm in a more existential mood than usual.

I feel like it's extremely grounded people who can decide, smack in the middle of their life, exactly how they should be reincarnated the next time around. I mean, I guess you really have to be pretty comfortable with who you are here and now to make concrete decisions about how you want to come back in your next life. (This is all, of course, predicated on the idea that we actually have a say.) And I feel solid enough with myself at this stage of the game that I think I've made my decision.

So after much thought and consideration, I've decided I'm coming back as a dog.

Now I've spent some real time over the past two or three hours kicking this around, and I really think that as far as reincarnation options go, a dog is the best choice. At least for me. Besides, my mother-in-law already hosied being a tall, blond bitch, so that's out. Too bad, too, because that would've been my obvious first choice. And a dog honestly seemed like the next best fit for me.

I mean, we're all coming back, so I might as well reconcile myself now to how I'm going to spend my next life. That way I can start making some plans. You know, get ahead.

Clearly, I love dogs. Always have. And since dogs are one of the world's most domesticated and popular animals, the likelihood of me finding a good home is high.

I haven't narrowed it down to a specific breed because I do actually feel like there should be some element of surprise. Like when you have a baby. You know you're having something, and you've got a fifty-fifty shot at one or the other, so you might as well wait until the big moment to find out what you end up with. As long as I know the basics, like number of legs I'll have and the relative type of food to expect, I feel like the rest is incidental.

Although, between us, that food piece is really my only stumbling block. Because I do love food so very much, and I'm not sure I can manage on a straight diet of Eukanuba. I may have to consider being a wild dog so I'll have more free-range options. Although that gets me into the feral dog community, and those guys are tough. They're like the Hells Angels of dogs. And I straight up refuse to rip out some other dog's throat just to get a chicken leg out of the trash. That's too barbaric for me. So I'm still weighing my options.

When I think about it, I can really see myself lying on a fluffy rug in front of somebody's fieldstone fireplace day in and day out. Preferably in Colorado. On a vista. With lots of land. In a log cabin with high ceilings and central air and a dog door built into the kitchen door. (I tend to go pretty deep into my own head on rainy days.)

I also love to snuggle and be scratched, which, in itself, represents a major percentage of a dog's life. And since my own kids have more or less outgrown cuddling with me, and neither one of them is apt to scratch me anytime soon, this is my shot.

And we haven't even talked about the running. Oh. My. God. The running! I could do it every day, all day. I could run rings around my past human self. I mean, I'd have twice as many legs, so just imagine the possibilities. And I'd be so sure-footed! I'd be like one step away from a mountain goat. And as long as I had flea and tick guard, I could run anywhere. Then, after I ran as far and as fast as I wanted, I could come home (conveniently slipping in through my little dog door so as not to disturb anyone), collapse in front of a roaring fire, and have someone snuggle and scratch me until I drifted off to sleep. Then I'd dream I was running. Because that's what dogs do. And when I was sleep-running, I'd whimper and kick my little hind legs, and my little human family would love me. Because everyone loves when dogs do that. They'd probably even love me more than my real family does when I do that now. Because when you sleep-run as a human, it's just considered bizarre and embarrassing.

I feel like I'm pretty low maintenance now as a human, and some of that would probably carry over into my dog life. I'm really good about keeping myself clean (although I'm not sure how I'd reach certain places without digits). I love to play catch. I love road trips. I think anyone who knows me knows I'd be sticking my head out the window all the way up to ski country if my kids would let me. And I'd be completely satisfied with a simple, yet colorful L.L. Bean slip collar. And maybe one of their premium, therapeutic, fleece-topped, memory foam dog beds. In plaid.

And I'm pretty good at occupying my time just thinking and observing life, so I think I'd be satisfied without needing to talk. I'm always up for a game of catch or Frisbee, and who doesn't love to roll around in the grass after it's been mowed? And if I can convince Dave to come back as a dog, too, then it's a win-win. Because I'm sure we'd end up being adopted by the same family. After all, there's a decent amount of karma factored into the afterlife, right?

So at the risk of being preachy, I'm suggesting you give your afterlife plans a little thought, too. You don't have to make any impulsive decisions, just kick the idea around for a while. And remember, tall, blond bitches and dogs are filling up fast.

Sometimes You've Just Got to Say Wtf

Printed August 2013

So these three ginormous scoops of ice cream are sitting next to each other, on top of a banana, in a fake plastic boat. The vanilla scoop says to the chocolate scoop, "Who the hell would be stupid enough to eat all of us at one time?" And the black-raspberry chocolate-chip ice cream scoop says, "Jeez, I dunno, but they'd have to be one helluvan idiot."

Famous last words, I guess.

That's what I'm sure my scoops of ice cream were saying to each other as my cousin and I started ripping into our three-pound banana split last weekend after a day at the lake with our kids. I'm not sure of the actual weight, but a three-pound ice cream sundae seemed like the right amount of drama to make my point. And let's just say that I felt like Adam Richman from *Man v. Food.*

Now I know what you're thinking. You're thinking, what the hell were you thinking?! (And that's without you even having a vague sense of what this thing really looked like. Otherwise you'd be saying that I'd lost my ever-lovin' mind.) And you're partially right. What the hell *was* I thinking? Because, truly, that much dairy and all those toppings and nuts floating around in one relatively small belly at the same time is bound to have catastrophic consequences.

But the pathetic irony is, I actually was thinking. And my thoughts were crystal clear. I knew exactly what I was doing, and although I proceeded with caution for obvious reasons, I went in eyes wide open. (Mouth, too.)

Funny, I know, because anyone who knows me well knows that I'm pretty disciplined about what I eat. I don't deviate much. I'm not like a food Nazi; I'm just mindful. Although my friends at work make fun of me (yes, you know you do) because I rarely if ever indulge in the fun goodies that parade around the office every day. They're all convinced that I never partake. Wrong. Wrong. Oh, so wrong.

What I try to explain to them is that I pick my moments very carefully, that's all. I indulge; just ask my family. I'm just very deliberate when I do it. That way it's more meaningful.

Like the time last winter on our drive home from ski country when I had it in my head that I needed a chocolate-covered coffee roll. (And yes, I do understand the difference between need and want, thank you very much.) I wanted it as much as I needed it. And although I rarely get that kind of a DEFCON 2-type craving (like once every two years), I take it seriously.

In this particular case, that meant swinging into every Dunkin' Donuts drive-through from North Conway, NH down to Ossipee. And there are many, trust me. Unfortunately for me and my poor thirteen-year-old daughter who I dragged along with me, there were no chocolate-covered coffee rolls left on the East Coast. Not my day. But as cravings will often do, mine forced me to get creative. And lemme tell you, desperate times can bring out the best and the worst in people. I'm not exactly sure which one it brought out in me, though. I'll leave it to you to decide.

At the last drive-through, I was given permission to stop by I ended up buying the only things they had left: a plain coffee roll and a Boston cream pie donut. Now here's the bizarre twist...I peeled off the top of the Boston cream and smooshed it onto the coffee roll. And voila! Best chocolate-covered coffee roll! Ever! And no, I haven't had one since. Haven't needed to. Craving satisfied. Problem solved.

See, I generally feel like too much of a good thing is usually bad. You know, all things in moderation and all that. I believe that being disciplined is good. In fact, it's necessary. But every once in a while, we just have to say, "WTF!" (And I don't mean Warwick Theater Fund.)

Every now and then we just have to be able to indulge and not beat ourselves up over it. And that's the key. We have to allow ourselves the right to eat the crispy extra-cheese pizza and the crinkly steak fries and a few of the beer-battered onion rings, and then maybe just a little taste of the bacon pizza (I mean it was right there in front of me). All without feeling like we've fallen ass over elbow off the wagon. Because if we're mindful and consistent most of the rest of the time, that's actually the ideal.

The expression "All work and no play makes Jack a dull boy" is floating out there for a reason. It serves as a reminder that we need to have the down to have the up. We can't have the black without the white or the coffee roll without the chocolate. They just don't work properly alone. Like if there were only one-way streets everywhere, everybody would be going around in circles. The universe needs balance. And the same goes for each of us as individuals. We're not supposed to only go in one direction without any turns. We'd just get dizzy and fall down. And where's the fun in that?

We need to fill the void every now and then. Because we're human. And cravings, in spite of the cravings-disappear-if-you-wait-twenty-minutes rule, need to be satisfied one way or another. Otherwise most of us can't move on. And we need to be able to move on. So that's why we're allowed, even encouraged, to have a treat from time to time. Because it preserves the natural balance of things and maintains a certain harmony.

So although I have no formal certification to grant anyone a license to do anything, I'm giving you my personal endorsement that you should feel free, every now and then, to indulge. I know we still, at least for a short time, have our bikini bodies to keep in mind, so just keep your head on straight and don't overdo it. And you know what I mean when I say that. Balance, people. Balance. I mean all things in moderation…even and especially the bad ones.

Back to School...We Got This

Printed August 2013

Before I say what I'm going to say, I want you to sit down. Or, at the very least, I want you to find someone or something sturdy to brace yourself against so when your legs buckle, you'll have something to grab on to. I'd never forgive myself if twenty thousand people collapsed and hit their heads all at the same time. The guys at the Fire Department would never let me live it down.

You ready? Here we go.

Summer's. Almost. Over.

Steady. Steeeeeeeeeadyyyyyy. OK. Breathe. In. Out. In. Out.

You still with me? Good. Look, we've all been here before, and we'll all be here again. The start of the school year works a lot like muscle memory when you're lifting weights. Even though we've been away from a routine for a period of time, our bodies and our minds remember how to go through the motions. And there's usually a small amount of initial pain, though, before we get our groove back.

Our amazing little brains have the capacity to store data and skills learned from the past in the form of emotion and memory. I'm not going to bother getting into the physiology of all the parts of the limbic system because then I'd be the one getting lightheaded and falling down. Suffice it to say, going back to school is like that first painful day back in the weight room—everything feels ten times heavier than usual, and it's the last place in the world you want to be. But we slog through it, and eventually it gets easier.

Feel any better? I didn't think so.

Let me put it all another way. Let's make it a numbers game. Maybe that will help.

So we've got over thirty-two hundred-plus kids in our little school system, spread out between eight schools. Now I'd love to be able to tell you exactly what that translates to in terms of actual number of families with kids in the system, but I can't. That's a tricky number to find. So because I have no choice, I'm going to guesstimate. And thankfully for me I'm not a news reporter, so my data can be completely skewed and it really doesn't matter.

Let's think of it this way: There have to be well over one thousand families living all around you, many of whom you know well, and every single one of them, in one way or another, is flipping out right now just like you. They're stressing and scrambling and shopping and panicking in all the same ways you are. But to me, that should be almost comforting. It means we're not alone. It's like death and taxes—we all agonize over them, but they impact every one of us no matter who we are.

Fortunately, in most cases, we have the ability to choose how we react to things. Even the things that panic us. We can choose to step up, or we can concede to fall down. We can decide to waste the next four days agonizing over reentry, or we can just say, "It is what it is," and reconcile with the inevitable. Embrace it even. Because when you think about it, it's much easier to digest something after you've chewed it up into little bits before you swallow it. A big bite of anything isn't quite so overwhelming once you've pulverized it into something squishy.

So that's what we're doing here. We're chewing. We're swallowing. And we're digesting.

It's like I always say to my girls, we can't always control what life throws at us, but we *can* control how we receive it.

So here's the plan (because I love a good plan): We all stay present in the moment until Monday night, sucking every last drop of summer out of Labor Day until we drain it dry. We focus on the now, knowing that the later is always a given.

Because, like it or not, Tuesday morning *will* come. The alarm *will* go off. And the nausea *will* swell up in your belly. But that's OK. It's expected. We just need to be prepared for it. We need to be able to anticipate and then to reconcile. We have to remember that back-to-school anxiety has existed since the beginning of time, when all the little cave moms used to stress about whether or not the antelope carcass would spoil before the second lunch block. We all go through it, and we all magically come out on the other side every time, in spite of all the anxiety.

As long as we acknowledge ahead of time that going back to school unleashes a bucketful of some crazy emotions, we can head them off before they take over. Kind of like a preemptive strike.

Because I honestly believe that if you get and maintain the upper hand in the back-to-school fight, you can win. Maybe not by a knock-out, but definitely by a TKO.

You can actually gain the upper hand in just about any situation with a set of good organizational skills and a little bit of prep work. In this case, we're talking about skills like premaking all your sandwiches for the week and storing them in the freezer. (That means no freezer packs needed in the lunch box.) Or setting the breakfast table the night before. Or having everyone lay out his or her clothes ahead of time. Or packing backpacks the night before school. Or labeling everything over the weekend and not on Monday night at eleven forty-five. It's these little things that give us control. And control usually trumps fear. And without fear, one is free to put one's head down, dig in, and get the job done.

So let's review. While thoroughly enjoying these last few days of summer, you're going to devote a modest amount of time each day to preparing for reentry. Think of it like stowing your personal belongings and putting your seat backs up and your tray tables in their upright position when you're anticipating a rough descent. You're doing all the little things you can do to make the landing smooth in bumpy conditions. This is not to say that you're not allowed to scream into your pillow when your alarm goes off on Tuesday morning. That's absolutely fine.

The main thing to remember is that the rabbit hole does, in fact, have an exit, in spite of how long and dark and frightening the tunnel might seem. Just take a deep breath, anticipate the other side, and start crawling. You'll make it to the other side, I promise. You'll be filthy and exhausted, but you'll make it.

No worries, right? You got this.

Popularity: Be Careful What You Wish For

Printed September 2013

First days of school can be interesting. Can't they? And when I say "interesting," I mean it in more than a few ways. There's interesting like watching a boy blow an eraser top out of his nose and across the cafeteria. There's interesting like the Texas gym teacher who wore the same outfit for picture day forty years in a row. And then there's interesting like how certain kids make it to the top of the popularity food chain while others don't.

And that's the interesting that I feel like talking about now that school's ramping up again. Because between you and me, that whole popularity enigma has baffled me since the first time I understood what popularity was back around junior high. And since I write about what I know—and I know plenty from my own experience as the kid who spent copious amounts of time wishing she had someone to sit with at lunch—here's what I know...

It doesn't matter whether you were the prom queen or the football captain or the kid who could never seem to find a gym partner, because I'll bet the farm that you've been touched in some way by social politics—as a kid, as a parent, or as a bystander.

I've spent a good part of my life fascinated by how people—kids in particular—can become so divided and classist at such an early age. Because, when you think about it, modern popularity as we know it is just the kid version of classism in its purest form. It's really nothing more than bias or discrimination based on differences made between social or economic classes—differences that usually come from nothing more than opinion, not even from fact. And in elementary or middle school, it could mean nothing more than not liking someone because he or she doesn't have a North Face jacket or a pair of Timberlands. Or, if you were me, it could be because you wore nothing but corduroy overalls to school most of the time. (I know, I know. Hindsight is twenty-twenty. I see that now.)

Just take a second and think back. Way back. Back to your first few days of junior high or high school. Try to isolate that moment when you first realized there were people around you who were perceived as popular or unpopular. Back to when you first recognized that people were secretly ranking you. Remember how powerful and intimidating that was? Remember that feeling of being judged and how hurtful it was? We all remember the people we thought could make or break our social status simply by giving us their attention or endorsement. Or by not giving it at all. There are certain things we never forget.

Ironically, these are usually the same people we had play dates with when we were kids. But somehow, suddenly, they became unapproachable. Abruptly and without warning, they cut the cord and let us drift away. These same kids who used to sleep on our bedroom floor in sleeping bags and fishtail braided our hair just cut us loose. Remember? You must, because it happened, on some level, to all of us.

Ever ask yourself why that was? Ever wonder how something as arbitrary as simple perception could have such power? God knows I have. And I'm astounded by it, even more now as a parent than when I was the unpopular kid going through it.

I can feel the ache of every kid who came before me and every one who's come since. Because that crazy enigma called popularity touches everybody.

But lemme tell you, the pain any of us felt as kids being the last one picked for the dodgeball game, or being the kid left without a lab partner or a bus partner or a table to sit at in the cafeteria, pales to the pain we feel watching our own kids go through it.

What I've learned is that popularity—or what we perceive popularity to be—is nothing more than an illusion. It's a sleight of hand,

and anyone can be fooled by the trick. I just hate seeing people get duped.

Maybe I've just got a little too much Martin Luther King Jr. on the brain. I really don't know. But I feel compelled as I watch another school year start to support the idea that change of any kind really starts at the grassroots level. It starts with us. It starts with dialogues with our kids and modeling and reinforcement and putting ourselves out there. And taking risks on people. And encouraging our kids to do the same.

I look at someone like Dr. King and the seismic impact that this one, single man had on the course of an entire civil rights movement, and I think that if one person can be so powerful to effect change, then imagine what an entire community or school could do if they were unified? Hmmmmm.

It's so important that we keep explaining to our kids that popularity is really nothing more than smoke and mirrors. We need to teach them that popularity—the way their generation perceives it—can be fleeting and random and dangerous. It's hurtful and can be lethal when put into the wrong hands. It's like chemical weapons for the heart.

Look, when you're ten or twelve or fifteen, you're finding your way. You're trying things on and seeing how they fit. And that includes attitudes. You're testing limits and learning how to push people's buttons for the first time. And there's a lot of power in that. So what we have to remember is that there isn't one of us out there—adult or kid—who doesn't wish to be popular.. But how we achieve that and to what degree are very impactful. Please don't let it cheapen the fact that Spiderman said this, but "with great power comes great responsibility." What we can't see when we're kids, unfortunately, is that popularity is really nothing more than a social phenomenon. And its randomness and fallout can be unpredictable.

That's why I think we need to stress to our kids, especially now that they're back in school, that how many friends they have in their circle or how many Instagram followers they have liking their feeds isn't a true measurement of popularity.

Instead we need to be pushing the idea that popularity should be measured by a person's ability to reach out to someone who *isn't* in their circle. It should be measured by how inclusive they are and how empathetic they can be. Like politics, I believe that popularity should be bipartisan, allowing everyone to coexist in ways that enable us to see what everybody has to offer.

I guess I just want us all to remind our kids, and then remind them again, that what they perceive popularity to be now isn't at all what popularity is really about. Popularity has evolved into a goal for a lot of kids. A pursuit. When what it's actually supposed to be is a byproduct of being a good person and making good choices. We have to remind our kids that popularity can be fake and fleeting and arbitrary. And what they should really be concentrating on is being real with people and being with people who are real themselves.

Because at the end of the day, that's who I want as my friend. And I can only assume that's who you want as yours and that's who they would want as theirs.

There's No 'I' In 'Team' For a Reason

Printed September 2013

I was not a confident kid. Not in my own head anyway. I know, I know, shocking. But true.

Put me on a soccer field or a basketball court or a lacrosse field when I was a kid, though, and I came alive. There was something about being on a team that just lit me up from the inside out. Probably because I was someone different when I was part of a team. The kids saw me as someone else. Someone of value, maybe. Who knows? All I know is that the playing field (pardon the pun) was leveled somehow when I was on a team. We all had a common goal, and we all worked together to achieve it.

When I put on that dank, ratty pinny, I turned into someone else. I became part of something special.

We worked together. We supported each other. We got to know each other in different ways, ways you couldn't always spot across a classroom. We had to. That's just what was expected, and everybody knew it. And although it was mostly unspoken, we all knew that those who didn't were out. So whatever anyone may have thought of me before or after the game just faded away for those four quarters. I was an equal. And I loved that. I embraced it. Probably because any insecurities I felt as an awkward adolescent kid just melted away when I took my place in that huddle. I was made to feel like I belonged there. And it was beautiful.

My teammates respected me for what I brought to the team. I may not have been the fastest kid out there, but they appreciated my effort. They knew I was always going to hustle because I loved the game—whatever the game was—and I was a competitor. They saw me as a mate. And little by little, over time, that transcended off the field and the court. And that changed me. And it changed my life.

Now I know that's not always the case. I know there are exceptions and there are kids out there who haven't had the same good experiences I've had. Everyone has moments that shake them. But I think, overall, most people you talk to who were either athletes themselves or have kids who are will agree that most of their experiences were positive. Most got something out of being part of a team and learning, firsthand, what that means. Learning that you have to make sacrifices for the greater good sometimes, even when it means giving up the ball to someone else. Learning that your way isn't always the best way and sometimes you just have to be a good listener and let yourself be coached. Because we're all a little narcissistic to some degree. And being put in a situation where it's not all about us is a good place to be sometimes. There's no better place to learn humility than out there on the court or the field.

We all know that all our kids, at some point or another, become completely egocentric. It's almost like a bizarre rite of passage that we, as parents, have to endure, just like our parents did before us. But when your kids are part of a team and forced to listen to an adult who isn't their father or their mother, there's a shift. Something happens. Egos are tempered. Attitudes are squashed. In fact, oftentimes our kids will respond better to an objective coach than they will to their own parent. And a dedicated and skilled coach can have an amazing impact on a child.

UCLA Basketball Coach John Wooden has said many brilliant things throughout his career, but when he said that sports do not build character, they reveal it, he reached right to the core of what sports means to me. When I heard that, he became my Muhammad, right then and there.

I've seen it with myself, transforming from an awkward tomboy to a more confident and solid young woman, just by virtue of being part of something that brought out the best in me. By virtue of strong coaches who led by example and modeled the kind of person I wanted to become. I got there by being forced to reach out to the other kids on my team and learning that there really weren't very many barriers that separated us after all. I see it with the young girls I coach. I watch them go from running around a track for the first time, breathing fire when they finish, to running a 5K race without stopping and still having gas in the tank at the end. I see it with my own kids. I see how the right sport fleshes out something in kids. It inspires them. It drives them in ways that academic success can't. It builds confidence and self-esteem. It teaches inclusiveness. It teaches them that being part of something larger than them has deep and lasting meaning.

I've watched my own girls scamper around the soccer field for years, loving it mostly because they were with their friends or because Dave was their coach, but not having that wild competitive desire to be the best in their sport. And then I've seen them find, by trial and error, a sport and a team that suited them. That embraced them. And the changes that happened as a result were magical. It ignited something in them. It drove them in directions they never knew they wanted to go. They never knew they could go. It drew them out and drew them in all at the same time.

So as far as I'm concerned, it really doesn't matter what sport your kids want to play as long as they play one. Encourage them to shop around and find the right match, because not all sports or all kids are created equal. Because it's only through being part of something bigger than they are that they'll truly be able to understand why the word "team" just doesn't sound right when you add an "I."

A Good Cleanse is Good for
the Body and the Soul

Printed September 2013

*I*t's important to note that this column was actually written last Saturday afternoon but is still totally relevant. So pretend it's last Saturday, will you? Please, continue...

I'm absolutely starving right now. Like ravenous. Borderline eat-your-own-forearm-off kind of hungry. That's because it's been something like twenty-two hours since I ate last—since my whole family ate last, actually. People are cranky. People are woozy and lightheaded. People are dazed and confused. People are hanging by a thread.

No, we're not doing the Look Better Naked Cleanse, although I am dying to look better naked and I love a good cleanse. We're fasting.

Why are we fasting? Because it's Yom Kippur and we're Jews, and that's what Jews do. We do it to clear out the mind and purify the body of everything we want to purge out of ourselves for the New Year. Our New Year. Our Highest Holy Day.

It's actually an amazing little tradition, this fasting custom; once you can get your mind around the fact that no food or liquid for twenty-four hours means no food products (not even gum) and no liquid, not even a drop of tap water for twenty-four looooooong hours. Real test of faith, this one. I highly recommend it, though, if you haven't tried it.

All right, hang on a minute, now I feel guilty. I've misled you. I'm not really all that hungry. This year's fast is really no biggie. We're eating in like two hours, and it went by pretty effortlessly for all of us, to be honest. I was overembellishing because I always feel like I owe you a compelling opener. So sometimes I may slightly inflate an idea to draw you in. Damn, now I feel dirty.

But you're here now, so you may as well keep reading.

I fast every year for a lot of reasons, the least of which is because I just love depriving myself of the deliciousness of food. Oh, food, I do love you. I do it because it's my people's Day of Atonement. I do it because it's a tradition. And because I believe in its fundamental purpose.

In case you don't already know the down and dirty about Yom Kippur, it's the day we, as Jews, have set aside to "afflict our soul," and atone for the sins of the past year. It's wicked dramatic sounding, I know. But for most of us, it usually consists of pretty low-level infractions like talking about people behind their backs or cheating on your time card or sneaking a small package of Hostess Powdered Donettes when you're supposed to be off the sauce. For some, though, the stuff they're dealing with is a little heavier and more life altering, like trust and fidelity and honesty and kindness. And that's because some of the stuff we need to look at when we look deep is deep.

So there's usually a lot of repenting and reflecting and goal setting throughout the day, and it runs the full gamut. But if you know me, then you know that all that stuff is right up my alley. And that's because I love an excuse to reflect and self-examine. That's because it usually leads to other good things like goal setting and action and change. Which I love, almost as much as I'd love some brisket and potatoes right about now.

There's a lot we can learn from fasting, lemme tell you. Not eating or drinking for twenty-four hours can be a pretty powerful exercise in self-control. There are some who say that fasting facilitates our ability to exercise discipline and endurance. And that's true, for sure. That if we can master our urge to eat for one day, well then, maybe we can have better control over our behaviors all year long. Maybe. That's definitely one reason to do it.

I mean, Muslims do it for an entire month for Ramadan. It's part of Hinduism. It's part of Buddhism. Even Christ fasted for forty days once. So there's obviously something to it.

Plus, it's good to want. And it's even better to want and not get. It's a great life lesson.

A good fast is designed to cleanse the mind and the body in one shot. And we all need that, more often than we realize. Going without food offers a certain perspective that we miss when we can just run to the fridge anytime we're hungry. It teaches us empathy for those who can't. It gives us a glimpse into a world where food is scarce or nonexistent. It puts the shoe, even for only a second, on the other foot.

Fasting is an opportunity—it's a time and a place dedicated to doing nothing but looking back over where you've been and looking ahead to where you're going. And while I believe that we definitely can't change the past, we can most certainly adjust our future. And an exercise like fasting can be a good teeing-off point.

Now, I'm way more spiritual than I am religious. But that's a column for another day. I believe that everyone, on some level, needs to jiggle their connection to their faith every once in a while to make sure that the connection is fully plugged in. Because over time the signal can weaken if it's not adjusted.

And I feel so strongly about that, that I actually look forward to this holiday for that exact reason. I love it because it allows us to hold down the power button and have the screen go black, leaving us totally unencumbered and focused while we look squarely at where we've been. And it gives us the opportunity to figure out how we can do better as we move forward. Because I think we need that.

So while I'm not suggesting that you convert (although we'd love to have you, and my rabbi would be thrilled), I am suggesting that you find and take advantage of the opportunities you have around you to step back and discover a new vantage point. A place that allows you to see things differently. Because it's those different perspectives that can sometimes lead to the clearest views. And when you can see the forest for the trees, you can focus on the bigger picture of what you're really looking at. And when you can do that, the sky's the limit.

And will you looky there, I spent so much time talking to you, that it's time to eat. Timing really is everything.

You Just Can't Win Sometimes, No Matter What You Do. But You're Not Alone

Printed October 2013

I love my job. I really do. Like real, true love. Working in a school, in the office, I think, has to be the best gig going. (Sorry to anyone who might ever be angling to replace me, but they're going to bury me in my chair if I have my way.)

I love what I do for the obvious reasons: the people and the kids and the fact that whenever I get to sing "God Bless America," there's never any expectation that I'm going to be on key. But even more than that, I love it because, as a writer, it's given me an unlimited amount of material to write about. Every day is something completely different, even in spite of the fact that most days have that *Groundhog Day* quality.

It's the topics that present themselves in clusters that I pay attention to the most. The patterns and common denominators that everyone seems to be struggling with at the moment. Those are the things that usually end up here. I guess I kind of think of my column as the Island of Misfit Toys, where all of people's quirky problems and situations can go to get sorted out and redistributed in ways that people will ultimately accept them.

Because when they end up here, it usually proves, in a pretty clear-cut, two-dimensional way, that what you're dealing with is not unique. It's stuff that we *all* deal with in one way or another. And people can draw strength from that. I know I do. Because nothing helps calm you more than hearing that everyone around you is dealing with the same ridiculousness that you are every day.

Take last week, as an example. Over the course of just one day, fifteen different, but equally exasperated, parents showed up at my reception window and told me different (but similar) stories about how their kids flipped a nutty all over the living room floor because they were overwhelmed and frazzled. Ten-year-olds, overwhelmed and frazzled. Something's radically wrong here. At that age, our kids should be worrying, at most, about lattice multiplication and times tables and maybe being able to buy a pair of those new black Nike Elite basketball socks. Not much else, in my opinion.

But so many kids today are having daily meltdowns, and they don't even understand why they're sobbing in puddles of their own snot. Many of them can't even express to their parents why they're so stressed or what they're even wound up about. And that's just because they can't. 'Cause they're like ten.

Think about it, how many times have you, grown-up that you are, just wanted to drop to the floor in the small appliances aisle at Target and sob because you had to be in eight different places at once, had no time to get anywhere, and hadn't even thought about what you're making for dinner and it's already six fifteen.

When you think about how wound so many of us are with all our commitments, just imagine what must be going on in these tiny bodies who so desperately want to do everything that everyone around them is doing. And, sadly, they're overcommitting to the point where they can barely function. And that's not good. It's not good for anyone, let alone a young child. Because when you think about it, a twenty-five-pound barbell is heavy for most people. But when it's put in the hand of a kid, it's almost impossible to lift. And I think that's what a lot of our kids are going through. They don't want to miss anything, so they're driven to overcommit, but because they're only kids, they're not capable of seeing the long-term picture of what their commitments mean. Because when you deconstruct the preteen years, it ends up looking like a perfect storm of hormones, puberty, overscheduling, peer pressure, and stress, all mixed into little preteen bodies.

I've got parents streaming past my office like a salmon run, telling me they're begging for mercy on a regular basis because their kids are falling apart at the seams. It seems that there's an entire-population of kids out there who are carrying around a whole lot of adult-sized stress about stuff like playing on select sports teams or not being part of someone's Bar Mitzvah collage on Instagram. (You know, the really important stuff.) They're buckling under the pressure of what should be fun kid's stuff. And it's barely October. So I felt compelled to intervene and maybe throw a spotlight on what seems to be a bit of an epidemic and, oh, I don't know, maybe try to fix it.

Unfortunately, though, as much as I'd love to be able to give you some stellar, brilliant piece of advice that fixes everything, I can't. What I *can* do is remind you that, as parents, we have the right and the obligation to intervene when our kids reach their breaking point. It's up to us to put on the brakes and set limits and just say no to playing three sports in the fall or doing four extracurricular activities just because they don't want to miss out. It's our job. It's our responsibility. And even though they'll hate our guts for it on the outside, they love us for it on the inside. They'll just never show it.

Because kids need limits. And they look to us to set them. And while I know that we're all desperate to be our kids' friends, we just have to accept that that comes later. And it will, I guarantee it. Just not now. It can't. There's a time and a place for everything, right? And right now, it's more important that you be your kids' parent than their friend.

Remember, you're never going to be viewed as the hero or the good guy or a buddy while they're young. No matter what you do or how well you do it. It's just a fact that we all have to accept. It sucks, but that's just the way it is. Right now you're the nasty !@^%##! who tells them they can't do what they think they want to do.

So what, my friends, do we do? How do we deal with these little stress balls melting down all over the kitchen floor every morning before school or every night before bed? How can we explain to them that what they're feeling inside is called anxiety? And that they don't need to put so much pressure on themselves to do everything that everyone else is doing? And how can we do it when they think that everything that comes out of our mouths is a load of crap? Interesting pickle we're in, isn't it?

Well, to be honest, you're damned if you do and damned if you don't. And that's the bottom line. It's not a pretty line, but it's all I've got. You need to reconcile that you just can't win, no matter what you do. But you must never stop. You can't. Because in reality, we're not supposed to win. We're just supposed to survive.

Remember, you're not allowed to tap out on this. We need to think of raising our kids like a steel cage match where no one gets out until the bell dings, which, in our case, is a good eighteen years (or longer, sorry). But what you're experiencing now is not what you'll be dealing with later. Remember that. Today's hell is tomorrow's vague memory (usually replaced with another, more complicated hell). But it does improve. They do get it. They do evolve. They do figure it out. And, believe it or not, they will thank you. And then, somewhere down the line, you can come and thank me.

Aunt Flo: Exposed

Printed October 2013

I don't use the word "hate" very often. I mean, it's so powerful and harsh and cold. Plus, it just conjures negativity, and you know how much I hate negativity, as a general rule. So you know when I use it, I'm not mincing words. I'm being very deliberate.

All that being said, I hate my Aunt Flo. I know that makes me sound like a terrible, awful person, but it's true. And I think, after thirty-plus years of dealing with her unannounced visits and disruptive nature, I'm finally ready to expose her for the nasty biatch she really is.

Clearly I'm personifying here, both for dramatic effect and to help you be able to better visualize something that's historically difficult for people to describe. But yes, in case there's any doubt, I'm talking about the hateful visitor we girls get every month. You know her, she's the one who renders most of us incapable of living normal emotional and physical lives one solid week out of every month. The one who makes the men in our lives want to fake a business trip every three weeks that "coincidentally" coincides with our Aunt Flo coming to visit.

If you haven't guessed by now, I'm talking about periods. Yes, periods. You know, "code reds," "cousin Claudia," "communists in the summer house," "time of the month," "the curse," "having the painters and decorators in," "lady days," "nature's gift," "the misery." And I'm doing it right out here in the open, where everyone can see me, with no veil of modesty whatsoever. But that's probably because I have relatively no fear when I'm typing words onto a two-dimensional computer screen. It's not usually until Thursday afternoons, when I read the paper and see what I wrote in print, that the reality of what I might have said hits me like a brick in the face.

Now my teenage daughters would be emotionally ruined if they knew I was writing about this publicly, but since they're both so completely absorbed in their own lives and barely, if ever, read my columns, I figure the over-under on them reading this is low. So just do me a favor, be a pal, and don't mention my column if you happen to see them anywhere.

Actually, I'm talking about this with a real purpose, as I try to do most things. And I feel pretty confident that most people out there can handle a conversation like this. We're adults, after all. And it's not like I'm swearing. I'm just using harmless little euphemisms. So before you write me off as a complete shock jock, just hang in there 'til the end. Because I'm confident (or at least hopeful) that you'll walk away with some kind of higher understanding of why I felt like this was an important thing to talk about.

It's because I try so hard to write about universal issues that seem to be the most mainstream at the moment that I just couldn't let this subject go unaddressed. I like to start dialogues that might somehow be useful on a global level. Things that have mind-shifting capabilities. And while I know that the chances are good that this subject has never been addressed here, like this, I figure if not now, when? And if my talking about it can give people a greater sense of calm and control over an otherwise volatile issue, then I'm compelled to forge on.

So let's forge.

I feel that lately I'm hearing a lot of ranting out there from girlfriends (and even some guys) about how upended they feel whenever "that time" of the month comes around. It seems like this one thing impacts nearly everyone, and not in a good way. I mean, most of us are just trying to get by on a good day, so when you factor in a full week of the month feeling bloated, ravenous, irritated, anxious, and moody on top of all the regular junk we deal with, it makes it a little tough to function normally. And I'm writing to the guys here as much as I'm writing to the girls because this affects you almost as much as it does us. So I guess I'm thinking it might be beneficial for the guys to really understand what's going on under the hood every three weeks so you have some shot at being able to survive the undertow.

Now I'm talking directly to you, guys…

Three weeks out of the month, we love you. The other week, we want to stab you in the throat. I'm sorry, I know that's tough to hear, but I'd rather you know the truth than be misinformed. Also, forget everything you've ever heard or read about how to handle a hormonal woman. Here are the top survival points, so focus: Do not speak unless spoken to. Because anything you say can, and will, be used against you. Hold all compliments until she's smiling at herself in the mirror again because that means the bloating has officially passed. Give her anything and everything she asks for. Do *not* ask questions. And for God's sake, no touching! Touching a menopausal woman is bad. B-A-D. And keep your fingers away from her mouth at all times. I know guys who've lost an index finger up to the knuckle because they got too close during our feeding time. And I call it "feeding time" because that's what it is when we have our period. Our eating turns very primal. If there was a carcass on the side of Atlantic Avenue and we were desperate and without kids in the car, some of us might actually stop to feed. Don't act overly happy around us; we hate when other people are happy when we feel miserable. Don't ask for anything. But that goes back to the not speaking, so if you remember that, you're covered. And keep the kids away, as much for your sake as for theirs. No interaction between a child and a hormonal mom will end well. There have been studies done, I'm sure. Oh, and did I say no sex? Or was that implied? Otherwise, that should about do it. Follow these instructions, boys, and you're home free.

Finally, to all my sistahs out there…

Didn't your mother ever tell you, you get what you get, so don't throw a fit? Well, that's really all I've got here. Remember, we can give birth, and that's amazing, right? Otherwise I've got nothin'. Sorry. Guess it just is what it is. Just thank God Midol is over the counter.

Why Do Haters Gotta Hate?

Printed October 2013

I know this might be coming a little out of nowhere, but considering the randomness of how my brain fires, anything can shoot out at any time. So for me, this kind of question is perfectly normal.

Let me ask you, in your opinion, do you think most people want to be successful? I know, it sounds kind of rhetorical and almost dumb to ask, but humor me. I'm asking because I genuinely feel, deep down, like most people do. And I'm guessing you probably feel the same way.

Why, then, have I been hearing chatter from so many people about issues they're having with haters hating them just for being productive and trying to do their jobs well? That just makes no sense to me. In fact, it seems almost asinine.

Now I use the word "hater" assuming that you spend as much time on urbandictionary.com as I do, and that you're totally down with what the word really means. But if you've got no idea what I'm talking about, then let me explain. A "hater," by definition, is someone who gets irritated when other people around them take initiative or take their work seriously and go above and beyond their job description.

Now a hater could be a work colleague, a classmate, or a friend. Anyone, really. It's just a catchall word for a person who simply can't be happy for someone else's success, so rather than be happy for someone, the hater goes out of their way to make a point of exposing a flaw in that person.

I know this might come as a complete and total shock, but a hater is usually a pretty negative person by nature. I know, I know, hard to believe. (I'm smiling now. And it's my supercheeky, sarcastic smile.)

But really, I just don't understand how someone could go through life like that—hating all the good and positive things that people around them are doing. Or, more importantly, why the hell they'd even want to. All that negative energy—it's gotta be like walking around with a cinder block swinging from your neck. Living with that kind of pessimism would just suck the life right out of me.

I've always thought we were expected to give our work at least 100 percent? I mean, that's how I was raised anyway. And I think it's probably a fair assumption that most parents out there aren't raising their kids to be underachievers. I mean, they don't teach us when we're in school to give the best 50 percent we've got, right? Teachers aren't like, "Hey, Timmy, great job on that fifty you got on your biology lab! Way to go, buddy!" I feel pretty confident that no boss would intentionally hire people with an expectation that they do a half-assed job. We're taught to work hard for the sake of working hard, for the sake of being productive, for the sake of being successful. It's really that simple. Or at least it's supposed to be.

The thing is, I keep getting wind of situation after situation where people are being criticized for wanting to excel at their work. For wanting to do the best they can for the people they're working for. And that's just cray-cray (which is urbandictionary.com for crazy). And the sad irony is most of the people who complain the loudest about other people going above and beyond are usually the very same people who, if they really put their backs into it, could be superstars. But they can't see that. Instead the only way they can survive in the world around them is to spend all of their time cutting down the people who really take their work seriously, instead of just digging in and doing their version of their best.

The problem is there are too many insecure people out there, and the depressing thing is they're so busy feeling threatened by other people and trying to make those people look bad, that they've lost sight of the fact that everyone has something unique to bring to the table and life isn't supposed to be a competition. Because to go through life feeling insecure about putting yourself out there to the best of your abilities is just a loss. It's a loss for the hater, and it's a loss for the people around them.

It seems like, for some, being a hater is almost a full-time job. Ironic that if they'd just quit bad-mouthing the conscientious people out there, they could actually become valuable and productive themselves.

Most of us, as well as I can recall, were taught to aim high, to go above and beyond, to give "it" our best shot. And we weren't taught to do that for the sake of one-upping anyone. But I know those one-uppers are out there. I'm not as naïve as I look in my head-shot. They're hidden right there in plain sight, pretending to have your back while they're criticizing you behind it. They're the climbers who'll step on anyone's head just to get a boost up to that next level. To get the praise and the kudos and the slap between the shoulder blades that they need to satisfy their own insecurities. But it shouldn't be about praise. OK, correction: I'd be lying if I said it wasn't nice to hear positive feedback every now and then. Because it is. And no one should apologize for liking that. But, and this is a big but, we should all be out there doing a good job just for the simple sake of doing a good job. For the sake of, oh, I don't know, pride and a sense of accomplishment. Because I don't know about you, but if my name is attached to something, I damn well want it to be something good.

And that's actually a good segue to one final thought, and that is that most haters don't even realize they're haters. They're just so wrapped up in their disgruntlement toward the hardworking people around them that oftentimes they don't even know they're hating. And that's sad. Because they're not endearing themselves to anyone by cutting down everyone around them.

Look, any way you hold it up to the light, "animosity" is a dirty little word. So I guess we all have two choices: (A) we walk up to the person doing the hating and we dope-slap them in the forehead and say, "Dude!!!" or (B) we take a deep breath and walk through their cloud of bitterness like we were just Simonized at the Lynnway car wash and let it all roll right off. Because at the end of the day, a hater's gonna hate. But we have the ability not to care. Don't know about you, but I choose B.

We Aren't Supposed to See Around Corners
For a Reason, But I'd still Like to

Printed October 2013

I have something I need to get off my chest. But I have to say, it's a little embarrassing, so I haven't been in a big rush to go public with it. I mean, I don't want it to change how you feel about me, so I've been torn about whether or not to tell you.

Sit down. Stand. It's your choice. I just want you to be in a good, stable position to receive semicontroversial news.

It may surprise you. It may not. Just promise me you'll be open minded and you won't judge me.

(Deep breath.) I desperately—and I mean desperately—want to be a superhero.

I know. Curveball.

But stay with me.

Now onto *why* I want to be a superhero. And this is the part that might surprise you.

Look, I'd be lying if I said the idea of slipping on a pair of red patent leather, knee-high Wonder Woman boots every day wasn't appealing, because it is. I am a girl, after all. And while I'm sure that being a legit superhero would totally buy me VIP seating at restaurants all over town, not even that matters much to me. For me, it's about the powers. Nothing more. (OK, fine. Maybe that and just a cute, red sequin skort with built-in Spandex. Something swishy.)

Everything else like the fame, the notoriety, and all the complimentary schwag is just incidental.

I just want the abilities. But because I'm not a hassa, like Superman who has like every power out there, I don't even care about having all the trendy powers he has (selfish bastard). I just want one.

I want the power of being able to see around corners. Which, for all you laypeople, is superhero for seeing the future. It just sounds more superheroish the other way.

I hope you don't think less of me because I didn't choose a power like healing the sick or bringing back the dead. I'm a simple girl, and I have a superlimited attention span, so one good power is really all I can handle. I don't chew gum and talk well at the same time.

OK, why the big buildup to my real point here? Because that's how I roll. I'm all about the big lead.

Look, the sad fact is I want this power for one very simple reason. It's not glamorous or sexy. It's for practical purposes only. And I want it for the same reason that all moms secretly want it, because it would be the single greatest weapon to help us fight the fight against our kids' number one, worst archenemy: *themselves.*

I can't tell you how many times I've tried, since my kids hit puberty, to explain to them in simple, easy-to-understand English that whatever crisis they were dealing with was not, in fact, the actual end of the world. That whatever fight they were in with a friend would actually resolve. That the zit on their cheek would eventually fade away. Or that, sooner or later, what goes around does actually come around.

If only we had the *power* to prove to them that we knew, for sure, that they'll make it through middle school and high school and beyond. That friends will come and go and come back again. That they won't always be sitting alone in the cafeteria at lunch. That, yes, you actually can make new friends at the middle and high school level. Or that they will, most definitely, figure out what they want to do with their lives.

Because I don't know about you, but my kids aren't buyin' it when I tell them that things almost always have a way of working out. And I could say it waving a stack of statistical data in their face that proves it, with Dr. Oz standing behind me giving the thumbs up, and they'd still shrug me off. I could bring in a panel of experts, buy them a book about it, read them an article, send in a dozen other parents to say the same thing, and they'd still think I didn't know what the hell I was talking about. But say it as a bona fide superhero with registered powers from the Justice League, and BAAAAAM! They can take that to the bank.

It's unfortunate that the parent-child relationship was designed with the genetic flaw that inhibits credibility with our kids, rendering whatever we say and however we say it useless. We're constantly swimming upstream against a current, with a bowling ball chained to our ankle, in a perfect storm. And that's exactly why I think that having this superpower would change everything. If I had the see-around-corners power and could *prove* to them that I'm right about everything I'm telling them, then I'd defeat the insecure, immature child that lives inside them and controls most of their rational thoughts.

I would win! Can you imagine?! They'd stop being their own worst enemy, and I could go on with my life instead of spending the majority of my time unsuccessfully trying to convince my kids that life has a way of working out. That tomorrow is always another day. I mean, it's exhausting, right?

So while I'm crossing my fingers that some kind of gamma radiation project goes awry while I just happen to be standing in a laboratory lobby, exposing me to a one-of-a-kind radiation cocktail that gives me my sweet, new superpower, I know the likelihood is low.

Guess I'm just destined to live my life like oh, I don't know, Lois Lane, and fight evil from behind a keyboard. But I refuse to give up hope. 'Cause you just never know.

The More Things Stay The Same,

The More They Change

T he more things stay the same, the more they change.
I know what you're thinking…crazy chick's got it backward. It's supposed to be "The more things change, the more they stay the same." But the truth is, I don't have it reversed. I'm saying it exactly how I mean it.

Why am I saying it? Because I had a revelation. I had a moment. And a pretty big one in the great scheme of moments.

It came at me from behind, like a sneaky little ninja moment. The kind that just tiptoes right up alongside you when you're looking the other way and then slaps you across the face. The kind that makes you feel like you must've been asleep at the wheel because it catches you so off guard.

My moment came when I was driving Carlos, my sixteen-year-old daughter (She hates when I use her real name.) and her friend home from cross-country practice. They were in the car making plans to go Halloween costume shopping later that night—plans that I just instinctively assumed would involve me, me being a licensed chauffeur and all.

So I was only half listening to them while they were hashing it all out, partly listening to "Royals" on Kiss 108, and partly thinking about the different ways I could prepare fingerling potatoes for dinner.

Now keep in mind, it was almost dinnertime and I'd been driving people around all afternoon, running errands, picking people up all over town, stopping home to switch laundry—the exact same thing I'm sure you were doing. So when they started talking about driving up to the Halloween store to look for costumes, I just fired off the ol' "N'Idon'tthinkso." Because, of course, short of hitching to get up there, I know I represented the foundation of their transportation plan.

It was at that moment that they both started laughing. And that's when I became totally confused. Because normally, when you shoot your kids' plan down right out of the clear blue sky, the last thing they're doing is laughing. They're usually distraught and giving you a whole lotta grief. But in my car, on that day, there was only laughter. Hence my confusion.

Now we're going to pause here for a minute. Because I think it's worth it, just for a second, to circle back to what I started talking about in the first place: Change. Specifically, change as it relates to the blissful teen years. (I think I just threw up in my mouth.)

I just need to say, for the record, that the split second we, as parents, settle into a relatively smooth groove of knowing what to expect from our kids, we should expect to get rear-ended by a big truckload of change. Because, for about a minute, things are predictable with our kids. And then, all of a sudden, the predictability train car derails; and before you know it, you're in a twenty-car pileup at the bottom of a ravine, and you're smack in the middle of a scene from *The Fugitive*. And that's what I'm talking about here.

Back to the story.

It was about now that the girls explained they were simply informing me, out of courtesy, that they were going to the Halloween store and then getting themselves, operative word here is "themselves," to their XC team dinner. To which I said, "Huh??????" And I'll admit, now that I think back on it, I did say it in a rather dumb-sounding voice that made me seem incredibly dense. But that's just because I was so used to the fact that they've always needed me, or another parent who had four wheels and a chassis, to go anywhere. And it's been that way for like, uh, ever. That's why it caught me totally and completely off balance that they had reached a point where they didn't need me like that anymore.

Now, I'm not gonna lie; I was a little thrown. So much so that I actually interrupted them and asked them to acknowledge the monumental event that was happening right before our eyes. I wanted them to witness, firsthand, the moment when everything changed for me. The moment when, out of absolutely nowhere, my daughter hit a whole new stage of independence. Well, semi-independence, really. It was her friend who was going to be driving them, since she was seventeen and cleared for takeoff.

It was right then, at that moment, that I had my epiphany that the more things stay the same, the more they change. And the realization stung. But only for a minute. (I mean I'm not heartless.) I did have a reflective moment, complete with a real-life flashback to all the buckling and unbuckling of car seats, followed by all the schlepping around of booster seats, followed by what felt like decades of driving to and from Kingdom Come. Which, by the way, is incredibly inconvenient to get to, especially from Marblehead.

So while there was a second or two of real, legitimate nostalgia, I reconciled with it pretty quickly. Partly because it just felt right. And partly out of necessity. You see, I'm a crier. And my kids give me tons of crap over the fact that I'll sometimes just look at them and start to well up. I mean, Jesus, I am a mother. But they refuse to cut me any slack. They nail me to the wall on it every time. So I'd be damned if I was gonna pop even one tear in front of them. Instead I turned to humor to mask any of the real emotion that might have been bubbling up under the surface. I asked them to take a pause and to focus on that one, simple little moment when everything changed for me. And what did they do? They laughed at me. Again.

But that's OK. I'm pretty good with change. That's why, while they were laughing, I mentally did my own little end-zone dance to celebrate what this all really meant: that I was gonna have a lot more free time on my hands.

So to all my besties, and you know who you are, slap that reserved sign on our table at Shubie's, 'cause my lunch calendar's got a whole lotta new white space to fill.

When The Going Gets Tough,
The Tough Get Going

Printed November 2013

I don't know about you, but with the crazy number of things we, as parents, could agonize over every day, I try to relegate mine to manageable fears like head lice, girl drama, my kids eventually having their own credit cards, and everything associated with my daughters dating.

Those are all realistic anxieties. Those are worries that we're trained to expect as parents. Those are the things we all anticipated when we signed on. They're the things we're equipped to handle, more or less.

So when I drop my kids off at school every day, I'm usually thinking pretty happy thoughts, assuming the fighting in the car has died down to just a jab in the ribs. Because I've learned to keep the other little fears we all deal with tucked safely in the back of my mind, behind a steel door that has no doorknob. They're there and I know it, but they're things I'm relatively prepared to handle; so it's easy to keep them in the background and not let them impact my day to day.

What I'm pretty sure has never crossed my mind, though, as I'm leaving the high school parking lot is "Wow, I hope my daughter's physics teacher doesn't get accused of trafficking child porn today."

I mean it's just not something the average parents think about as they're pulling away from the curb in the drop-off circle.

As parents, we expect to get hit with the puberty years and the raging hormones and the peer pressure and maybe some low-level lying. We expect that our kids might stay out too late without calling or ride their bikes without a helmet or maybe exceed their texting limit, ten to twenty thousand. So as a result, we teach our kids appropriate coping skills and how to make smart decisions. We teach them what to do if a strange man asks them to help him find his lost puppy. We teach them how to stop, drop, and roll and how to just say "no" and not to be a bystander when someone's getting bullied.

These are all things we can prepare them for. These are things we can prepare ourselves for. But no one can be prepared for the news that their child's teacher abruptly left the classroom smack in the middle of a lesson to face felony charges of possession and transfer of child porn. Like what does a parent do with that? What does a school do with that? What does a kid do with that? I mean, there's no way a school can screen for that if someone has no priors. There's no hiring committee that can flesh that out of someone during the final round of interviews. Not unless the school committee approves waterboarding during the hiring process. And I'm guessing that's highly unlikely.

So although that leaves us somewhat susceptible to frauds, it doesn't leave us powerless.

Because in a world where school shootings and bombings and terrorism and teacher scandals are more mainstream than ever before, we could all very easily be paralyzed by the simple threat of these things every day. But we can't be. And I guess that's really my point here.

I've heard a lot of chatter this week about the high school teacher—Riley's teacher—who was clearly not who he represented himself to be. I've heard it from her, from her friends, and from other parents, and the one thing that resonated above anything else was that this guy who everyone trusted and took at face value may be one of the bad guys.

We were duped. We all were. And it was unavoidable. And that hurts.

But, sadly, there's no real way around being duped in a situation like this. Until such time as we can effectively read people's minds—at which point I'm completely screwed—we have no choice but to take people at their word. We have to assume that people *are* who they say they are.

And I know that that can be a little frightening, especially in light of all the scary things out there like terrorists and bombers and pedophiles and other SVU types.

So that leaves us with one clear choice of what to do. We have to remember that events like this that hit so close to home can have hidden benefits. They heighten our awareness. They unify people. They strengthen our resolve and move us to look out for each other and take better care of one another.

Because we can't live in fear of the scary things. The bottom line is we need to have what my husband Dave calls "a healthy fear of the really scary stuff," such as the one he says our girls get when they watch too much *SVU*. And my brilliant husband is absolutely right. We need to accept the idea of what *might* be out there and then compartmentalize it in a tiny drawer in our brain that locks with one of those cheap lockbox keys. And then we have to move on, armed with the knowledge that we're not gonna let anyone come into *our* house and push us around.

We have to remind each other and ourselves that the good guys far outweigh the bad guys in the world. And that all of us who are one of the good guys are all playing for the same team, and we need to have each other's backs.

Because let's face it, most people can't function well when they're excessively paranoid. And that's because paranoia is a wasted emotion. It messes with your head and leaves you looking pathetic. Not to mention the fact that you just can't accomplish much of anything when you're in a paranoid frame of mind..

So here's the thing, we all just need to use what happened at the high school as a reminder that we still always need to assume the best while being secretly prepared for the worst. And if that means all of us need to watch more *SVU* reruns, then so be it. Because when the going gets tough...the tough get going! Now who's with me?!

Don't Ever Look A Gift Horse In The Mouth

Printed November 2013

I love presents. I mean, who doesn't? It's a present. Just the simple nature of it makes you love it. It's the anticipation and the unwrapping and the shaking and the guessing. It's all just a big bunch of goodness.

But as much as I love them—especially the ones that come loaded with diamonds (Dave, that one was for you, babe)—I learned a long time ago that gifts come in lots of different shapes and sizes. And the good ones aren't just relegated to the little powder-blue box with the white ribbon, either. They come in lots of different forms—forms that we don't always recognize as gifts the first time around. That's why I always try to pay attention so I won't miss one when it comes in disguise.

Kind of like the one I got last week when I was waiting in the checkout line at CVS. And good thing I was paying attention, lemme tell you, because this one was a humdinger!

Now, I'll never divulge the name of the person who gave me this gift, because, quite honestly, names are irrelevant here; it's the story that's the real gem, so pay attention.

Let me frame it out for you.

I'm waiting in line to buy my three-hundred-count Excedrin bottle (I've got teenage daughters, what can I say?), when I glance over my shoulder and notice a friend of mine at the register next to me.

I say 'hi' and we chat for a bit, and then, as we're about to go our separate ways, she asks me if I can spare a minute to talk. What followed was a conversation that I could never have been prepared for in my wildest imagination. It both took me by surprise and inspired me in ways I'm still processing over a week later.

She starts by asking me if I remember back to the first time, many years ago, when we first met. And much as I wish I could remember it, I can't. So she reminds me.

My friend tells me that the first time we met our kids were all young, like elementary school age, and we were in one of the school parking lots waiting for soccer practice to end. Apparently, and unbeknownst to me at the time, I was parked in a handicapped spot. Now this detail alone was enough to throw my hands over my mouth, because I was so horrified at the idea that I was parked in a handicapped space. And that's because anyone who knows me knows that the only way you'd ever find my car parked in one is over my own cold, dead body.

But that's only a minor detail in the story. There's more. Oh, there's more.

She reminds me that my car was filled with kids and I was on the phone when she knocked on my window. She was knocking only to let me know, in case I didn't realize it, that I was parked in a handicapped spot. She wasn't there to yell at me or to chastise me; she was simply pointing it out.

But here comes the shocker...

It seems as though, after she pointed out where I was parked, I leaned out the window and said, "How do you know that I'm not handicapped?"

At this point my heart is a single pump away from exploding all over all my other organs. I'm horrified. Even the simple thought that such a thing could ever or would ever have passed through my lips has my mouth completely bone dry. I'm talking like a visceral reaction here—legs are buckling, hands are shaking, the full Monty.

Seeing how affected I am, she immediately says she isn't telling me this to upset me, but that it's part of a bigger story. She goes on to tell me that at that moment, her impression of me was cemented in stone. I was a bitch. And Jesus, I can't say I blame her.

She also acknowledges that I had a lot going on around me in the car that day and that it's possible I didn't hear exactly what she said. And we all know I've been known to be slightly sarcastic from time to time. Still, there would never be a legitimate excuse for that kind of a response. But be that as it may, I took her at face value and prayed to God there was some kind of mix-up in the universe that day and it was a case of mistaken identity. Either way I had absolutely no memory if it, nor would I ever have imagined answering someone like that.

She goes on to tell me that she's hated my guts ever since. BAAAAAAM! I took that one right between the eyes. She says that I may not have even realized it over the years, but she's made a conscious effort to avoid me. She even admits that she's read some of my columns and thought I was fake and a hypocrite. And hell, if I said what she thought I said, I'd consider myself a monster, too.

But here's the point where things took an unexpected turn. She tells me that she's confiding all this in me because she's had a complete revelation over the last few years and she felt it was time I knew.

You see, our daughters know each other well, and she's been more or less forced over the years to get to know me, too. And because of that, she's realized over time that the person she met that day in the parking lot was not the person she thought I was. She had what I guess you might call an epiphany.

And that's when I started to get choked up, right there in the express line. Because it was her honesty and her humility that really touched me. I mean let's face it, not many people would have the courage to admit all that. And I think even fewer still would've allowed themselves to change their opinion. But she did. And it was beautiful.

Now, you can bet that I gave her one helluvan apology just in case whatever did come out of my mouth that day even slightly resembled what she remembers hearing. But the funny thing is, she told me that an apology wasn't necessary because karma had already balanced the scales years ago.

Apparently, shortly after that day in the parking lot, I fractured my ankle running. So the next time she saw me I was on crutches. And she said she just smiled when she saw me, because she knew at that moment that karma had evened the score. And I really didn't blame her for thinking it, either. Because I guess I would have too, if I were her. And I admired her for saying it to my face.

We hugged before we left the store, and I meant it when I told her how grateful I was that she finally told me what had been on her mind all these years. It was a brave move, and I respected it.

So what's the lesson in all this? Well, I think it's pretty obvious. Don't ever look a gift horse in the mouth, because you just never know what's gonna be inside the box. It might just be the best thing you never knew you wanted.

Sometimes, You've just gotta take the Road Less Traveled

Printed November 2013

Let me be the first to admit that I love the status quo. No one's happier than me when all my duckies are in a nice, neat, little row.

You want the truth? Predictability excites me. Kind of like how a wrecking ball excites Miley Cyrus. I can't help it. I like my keels even. And I'm usually happiest when my life is like a nice, long, flat stretch of autobahn, where I can open it up and get all Mario Andretti if I feel that need for speed, or I can just flip on cruise control, sit back, and enjoy the ride. I guess I'm just a simple farm girl at heart, what can I say?

All that being said, there's also a part of me that likes to mix things up and go off road. Farm girls have to be rugged too, you know. A girl's gotta be tough to handle all those cows and chickens, after all. Because as much as I'm a lover of habit and routine, there's a side of me that loves to double clutch and jump the guardrail. And that's because I also believe that sometimes the best trips happen when you throw your life into four-wheel drive and go off your own grid.

I'm saying all this because my family just busted out of our wheelhouse and threw most of our predictable little family routine right out with the trash. We put ourselves out there, and what we got back in return blew every single one of us completely away.

You're dying to know how; I can feel it. And I'm dying to tell you. So enough with the metaphors. In straight-up English, here's how we took the road less traveled and where it took us.

Our journey, for lack of a better word, started the night one of my daughter's friends needed a place to stay. Riley's friend—a senior and fellow cross-country and track runner—has spent the better part of the last eleven years commuting from Boston to Marblehead every day to get her education. So when the late commuter bus leaves and she's not on it, she'd better have a backup plan.

Now I'm sure you don't need me to describe what her typical day to day looks like. You get the concept of commuting, so you can deduce. Although, just in case you're at all vague on what it means to live eight towns away from your high school, her typical day goes something like this: Up at 4:30 a.m. Jam everything you could possibly need for that day into your backpack and pray you don't forget anything. An hour on a bus. A full school day. A two-hour cross-country practice. Back on the bus for another hour. Dinner. Homework. Shower. Bed. Repeat. For eleven years. Almost a mirror image of what life is like for our kids, no?

So the night the team dinner ran late and she needed a place to crash, we said sure. Little did we know that that one night would evolve into many nights. And those many nights would grow into weeks at a time. And eventually, it would turn into a virtual adoption into our family. Complete with toothbrush, lunch box, and a pink pair of feety pajamas if I can find them in her size.

Now keep in mind, until this point my daughter's friend was only someone we knew through school sports. She was a friend we rang the cowbell for during a race, gave rides to in a pinch, and high-fived when she ran her personal best. But as being a part of a team can often do, it unites people in very unexpected ways. And it was because of the bond they'd formed that we were happy to have her stay.

So I guess, at this point, you could say that we were still driving on a pretty freshly paved stretch of highway. What none of us realized was that the highway was about to end, and we were all about to go screaming off the cliff *Thelma & Louise* style.

At first when she stayed with us, we all treaded lightly, observing each other, sizing each other up, and crunching over a few eggshells along the way. But before long, and without even realizing it, we wove ourselves into each other's patterns.

She started making my coffee just the way I like it. I learned that she likes Craisins in her salad, but not too many as to overwhelm the rest of the veggies. Because life and salads are about balance. She learned where things were in the house even better than Dave. (Sorry, babe, but the Q-tips have been on the same shelf in the same closet for ten years.)

She floated her way into our little morning breakfast ballet, knowing exactly what everyone's choreography was, when to dodge and when to weave, when to duck and when to cover.

The girls all began doing their homework together, carpooling together, gossiping together, counseling each other, and, most importantly, having each other's backs.

And the irony of all this is that while we've been acting as a support system for her, she became a support system for us. She brought out the best in all of us. And I'd like to think we're bringing out some of the best in her, too.

Janaya is graduating in June and moving on to the next phase of her life. And I'm already getting choked up while I'm typing this. Damn. I have such a week emotional constitution. But because we all put ourselves out there so many months ago and barreled headfirst into the complete unknown, we'll always stay connected. We're part of each other now and I feel pretty sure that that will never change.

So I guess this just proves my point that you never know what you'll get out of something until you put yourself out there, step outside your sweet spot, and really open yourself up. Even, and especially, if that means busting through the sawhorse in the middle of the road and ignoring all the flashing lights.

Oh, Thanksgiving, How I've Missed You

Printed November 2013

I'm so excited! I'm so excited!! *I'm so excited!!!* I can't wait for to-morrow! I can't wait for tomorrow!! *I can't wait for tomorrow!!!*

I'm sure it's tough to read between the lines here, but in case you couldn't tell, I'm like practically jumping out of my skin that tomorrow is Thanksgiving. And that's because tomorrow, above all other holi-days, is my absolute, positive, most favorite day of the year. It trumps everything for me. Even my birthday and Hanukkah. Although this year, I'm getting a twofer because Hanukkah just happens to fall directly on top of Thanksgiving. Shaaaazaaaam!

Now keep in mind, you're only experiencing the one-dimensional version of my over-the-topness over Thanksgiving. There are at least two more whole dimensions that my family and friends have been stomaching for the last week, so be glad you can just wad up the newspaper and toss it in a basket. They're stuck with my crazy 24-7. And believe me, it's a whole lotta crazy.

About a week before the Big Day, I start humming incessantly and pretty much keep it up straight through Thanksgiving dinner. (Yes, I hum even while I eat. I get that from my mother. Genetics.) It's no picnic to be around either, just ask my kids. But I'm happy as hell, so who gives a damn?

I suppose it sounds a little kooky that one, single day that involves endless hours of food shopping, prepping, cooking, serv-ing, and cleaning is such a big day for me. Especially when I'm the one responsible for most of the food shopping, prepping, cooking, serving, and cleaning. But it is. And it always has been. In fact, I get giddier about it every year. Giddier and, of course, more nostalgic. Especially as I watch my kids grow up from little peanuts who needed a booster seat at the table to the beautiful young women they've become who now actually help me shop and prep and cook and serve and clean. (It's good to have cheap child labor.)

You see, for me, Thanksgiving is all about one thing: the people who mean the most to me being under the same roof, telling the same stupid stories, running the same Wild Turkey five-miler, screaming for our Magicians at the Thanksgiving Day football game, and making another year's worth of memories.

Now don't get me wrong, my supreme love of Thanksgiving by no means cheapens my excitement for all the other holidays. I love them all, for sure. But there's just something so special about Thanksgiving.

There's something about *this* day in particular that touches me. It has a unique quality to it that none of the other holidays have. I suppose if I had to put my finger on it, I guess I'd say that what makes it so extraordinary is that it embodies everything that's really important and beautiful in life: family, friends, food, and football. Because, to me, those are the things that matter the most. (Not necessarily in that order, though. If the Pats are on prime time on Thanksgiving Day, then football sidesteps everything else into first place.)

Now I know that there are people who prefer to host the holiday and people who would rather be host*ed*. And thinking of it in terms of the chicken and the egg, they're both essential—you obviously can't have one without the other.

For some, that means enjoying Thanksgiving in an easy chair, beer in hand, feet up, with a dinner plate balanced on their knee, watching the game. And those people are critical to the Thanksgiving landscape because they're the foreground. While the others—the mixers, choppers, slicers, and servers—compose the background.

I honestly think people are born instinctively knowing which side of the table they belong on: the serving side or the receiving side. Because everyone has their sweet spot where they feel the most comfortable. And you can't paint a true Thanksgiving scene without both sides.

Me, I was born and bred to be a host. It's hardwired into my DNA, coming straight from the top down in my family. My grandmother hosted until she passed the baton to my mother, who eventually, once I was The Mom, passed it down to me. But not before a ten-year detour at my mother-in-law's house until my in-laws retired to Florida. Then it was mine. Mwaaaaaaa-haaaaaa-haaaaa!

I waited for that baton for decades, frozen in the starting position with my arm extended behind me, just waiting to feel that holiday pass into my hot little hand. Because I knew that when I finally got it, I was going to run with it as long as I had breath left in my little lungs. And that's probably because, for me, hosting Thanksgiving was more of a coming-of-age than anything else. It was a marker. A milestone. It was finally my chance to say "thanks" to the people who mean the most to me for "giving" me a beautiful life.

Look, the people who end up around my Thanksgiving table are the ones who mean the most to me in this world. And I'm sure, for the most part, the same is true for you. They're the grandmothers and the grandfathers and the mothers and the fathers and the sisters and the brothers and the aunts and the uncles and the cousins and the friends who make our life beautiful. They're the ones who've seen us at our best and put up with us at our worst. For me, they're the people who've watched me laugh so hard I actually wet my pants and the ones who've wiped away the tears on my worst of days.

That's why this day, this Thanksgiving holiday, is the purest holiday of all. There's no biblical basis to it whatsoever. There are no rites or rituals. And no presents to buy. Only the traditions born from each family that mark the way they celebrate this day—a day that's designed to let us relish everything that's good and right and bountiful and oval and pig skinned.

Thanksgiving produces an organic kind of happiness—a happiness that comes from the simple enjoyment of people, of food, and of football. And if you happen to be in my house, a joy that comes from endless hours of cutthroat Boggle. It's like steel-cage-match

Boggle, a modern version of gladiator combat where throats are slit and bodies are disemboweled all in the name of sport. What can I say, it's our tradition.

But most of all, Thanksgiving is a day designed to celebrate the essence of life. Which, in case you didn't already know, is people. Because none of us walks through life alone. We all have partners along the way—people who steady us and keep us on course, people who pick us up when we fall, and people who lead us when we're lost. And it's these people who make the journey worth taking.

So as you sit around your tables tomorrow and look at the faces around you, take a minute, and thank them for helping to give you a beautiful life. I know I will. Then pass the potatoes, will you?

Thanksgiving May Be Over, But Your Next Cheat Day Is Just Around The Corner

Printed December 2013

OK, Thanksgiving is over. It's a big buildup and then, kind of suddenly, everything stops. A lot like childbirth.

By now the turkey carcass is double bagged and waiting at the transfer station to be incinerated. Most of the out-of-towners have caught their Acela train or made their JetBlue connections. And the first official round of the holiday season is over.

I find that it's usually around this point, after the chaos of Thanksgiving has passed and leftovers have dwindled, that most of us emerge from our little gluten bubble and realize just exactly how far off the wagon we've fallen. And that realization is generally pretty ugly.

It usually starts the morning after everyone leaves. In the bathroom. When you're alone for the first time and you confront yourself in the mirror. And your pissed-off reflection looks at you and yells, "Oh! My! God! What did you just do?"

This is that point where people (OK, fine, women) start tabulating, in the form of calories and serving sizes, the amount of actual damage we did to our GI tract in only four short days. Bloated and cranky people everywhere wake up to the reality of what they did while they were binge eating over the long weekend. And for most, it feels like a dope slap with a cricket bat.

I think it's a safe bet that the majority of women everywhere spent the first part of this post-Thanksgiving week shell-shocked in their walk-in closets. Each one of them trying to button their skinny jeans, knowing that it's impossible to jam a square peg into a round hole. And alongside them is a pretty good-sized population of guys tossing on their elastic-waist sweatpants, shrugging, and working from home until they can fully exhale inside their suit pants again.

When we're in the thick of it, swept away by the fervor of the holiday and the smell of the food and the deliciousness of the pumpkin whoopie pies, most of us slip into a different state of consciousness. We're thinking and talking and carrying on seminormally, but there are certain synapses in our brains that stop firing. I don't want to say we become zombies because that's a little too farfetched, even for me, but you get what I'm saying.

Since Thanksgiving is primarily about eating and socializing and watching football while we eat and socialize, a portion of our brain instinctively turns off, allowing the enemy holiday food to overtake us, kind of like when the force field around the Death Star went down and gave Luke Skywalker and his Jedi bros unrestricted access into the belly of the beast.

During the Thanksgiving break, we stop thinking like rational, calorie-conscious adults. We submit and then we consume. It's the nature of the holiday. But I think people tend to forget that that's exactly what we're supposed to do. Exactly like when bears prepare to hibernate, they ingest everything they can find for a given period of time. And we do it for the same reason the bears do—we eat without restraint because it's really our last chance for the winter to legitimately overindulge. The only difference between the bears and us is that we do it by aligning our gorging with a major holiday while the bears do it for survival. Gotta love having opposable thumbs. Homo erectus all the way, baby!

But what I think everyone needs to remember is that the nature of Thanksgiving is to celebrate and indulge and give thanks that there are seconds and thirds to indulge in. I mean that's the point, right? Thanksgiving is about cooking food and eating food—as much as we want for a finite amount of time or until we throw up. Whichever comes first.

So don't beat yourself up too badly over whatever you did at the dinner table. It's OK. It's expected. We all did it to some degree. And you're probably not set back as far as you think you are, assuming you've stopped eating by now. (If you haven't stopped yet, now would be a good time.)

Remember, we're all pretty much in the same boat, albeit a sinking one because our collective weight limit is way above maximum capacity.

In our defense, though, most of us at least try to maintain some kind of routine and consistency and nutritional balance throughout the year. We're conscious of what we eat and of getting to the gym or of taking a run or of catching that spin class. We try. We try hard. We schmear the peanut butter on the celery. We opt for the egg white omelet instead of the short stack of pancakes. We try to make good choices. And why do we do this? To be able to cheat on our predetermined cheat days, of course.

Even the strictest diets and nutritional plans account for a cheat day every once in a while. So don't beat yourself up too bad over that second piece of pie or that fifth chocolate chip cookie. Thanksgiving is just one of calendar's built-in cheat days.

I mean, hasn't it dawned on anyone but me that all of the major holidays are strategically staggered a month or so apart throughout the calendar year? Those Founding Fathers were *way* ahead of their time. Holidays are built-in cheat days designed to give you something to look forward to and enable you to stay on track all the other days in between.

Look, we're all just mere mortals who can't be expected to resist the temptation of my mother-in-law's crème squares, especially when they're on a platter right next to my chewy molasses cookies, which just happen to be diagonally across from the warm apple pie. No one's that strong.

Because as bad as you binged and as poochy as you feel, what you have to remember is that you're only ever one meal or one workout away from being right back on track. And that knowledge, while not quite powerful enough to eradicate unwanted calories and shrink pant sizes, can offer a little solace when you're trying to regroup and find your way back on track.

So don't be too hard on yourself, you've just got to hold it together until Christmas, because after that it's only a sneeze until Valentine's Day. Eye on the prize. You got this.

When It's Holiday Time We Push On,
Because It's Just What We Do

Printed December 2013

So I'm feeling a little guilty and I need to purge a little to clear my conscience. Never mind the fact that whenever I need to come clean about something, I do it to roughly twenty thousand people. That's completely irrelevant. I realize that most normal people write in these little things called diaries when they're feeling especially guilty or emotional, but not me. Guess that makes me some kind of an exhibitionist. Oh well.

Back to why I'm feeling guilty.

I guess, if you peel the onion back to the core, I'm guilty because I'm a Jew. Relax, it's not because of the whole pharaoh and Exodus thing. It's a little more benign than that.

I'm feeling a little guilty because Hanukkah is over and I'm D-O-N-E, done with everything holiday related. And so are all my people. While most everyone else is not. And for the last few days, I've been watching everyone else I know scramble around in that kooky little Bermuda Triangle place between Thanksgiving and Christmas. And everyone's racing 100 mph for the finish line and trying to stay upright when they break the tape.

And it's a haul. I get it. I just finished wading through the same madness. So the feelings are all fresh.

But now that I'm on the other side of it, relaxed and with most of my faculties still intact, I really have only one thing to say: "Na-na-na-ne-naaaaa-naaaaa."

OK, that was childish. I'm sorry. I should be more supportive of the stress you're under as you scramble around trying to do all your holiday shopping and wrapping and hiding. But the circumstances are so unique for me this year with Hanukkah coming so early and me needing to do all my shopping back in August in flip-flops and board shorts. I'm really pretty much left sitting here with absolutely nothing to do. I mean, what are my choices now? Fold laundry and scoop out the ashes in the fireplace, or sit here with a cocktail and make fun of your nightmare? I mean, cummon. The choice is obvious.

The whole Hanukkah-falling-directly-on-top-of-Thanksgiving thing was just nothing I could be prepared for. Never saw it coming. (Clearly I spend most of my time in the here and now and not flipping through annual calendars of years that haven't even happened yet.)

Usually I set my holiday shopping deadline for Thanksgiving. That way, everything's bought, wrapped, and in a secure, undetectable location before we start stuffing the turkey. Bing. Bang. Done. But this year, everything was off. Because of this bizarro blip in the Jewish calendar, I practically had to back everything up to Labor Day. Which, at the time, seemed totally ridiculous. I mean who shops for turtleneck sweaters and Uggs in August? It just didn't seem right. But what choice did I have? The calendar says what the calendar says.

But now that my holiday has come and gone and my personal cloud of shopping madness has lifted, I'm honestly feeling pretty damn good. I'm not going to lie to you. I whistle now when I go anywhere. And when I think about going to the mall over the next few weeks, I imagine myself meandering around aimlessly, sipping my skinny peppermint mocha, watching the chaos swim around me. It's liberating, really. It feels like what I'd imagine running naked through a field of high grass would feel like. Not that I've spent much time fantasizing about tall grass and running naked. But at least that gives you a frame of reference.

Understand, I'm not saying any of this to taunt you. Well, not blatantly anyway. I'm actually trying to motivate you to keep pushing on, even when you feel like you can't stomach another trip to Target. And that's because pushing on is just what we do. You just have to take solace in the fact that, like me, you'll eventually check everything off your list, and the madness will end. I promise. And you'll have a whole 364 days to relax and unwind.

Look, it's what our parents and their parents before them and their parents before them all did. Someone did it for them and they did it for us and we do it for ours. It's almost like a rite of passage to endure the holiday season, especially when you're a parent. Because God knows none of us are really doing it all out of the sheer joy of schlepping to the Burlington Mall on Black Friday at 2:00 a.m. and waiting in a two-hour line just to get a ticket to get into the Apple Store to buy the pink iPad Mini.

We do what we do for our kids during the holiday season for one reason and one reason only, because we love them. We do it to see their faces and to share, even for a second, that feeling of sheer joy when they get exactly what they wanted when they tear open that box. Because we all remember what that feels like. And every one of us longs, in some way, to re-create that thrill and that feeling of magic and wonder. Because it's beautiful and it makes everything that we all do behind the scenes worth it for that brief moment in time.

So when you feel yourself getting short tempered and cranky and exasperated over things like wrapping paper and cookie swaps and crowds and lines, just remember who you're doing it all for and that you're in the home stretch with the finish tape in sight. Don't forget that you're doing it all for the people who matter the most. And that, at the end of the day, you wouldn't trade all the chaos and stress you're feeling right now for anything in the world—except maybe a quiet beach, a chaise lounge, and an open tab. Nah, not even that.

And just think, after it's all over, you'll have at least a good twenty-four hours to relax on Christmas Day before you've got to pack up everything you just bought and hit the return line. Or you could've just converted. Then you'd be done by now.

When One Door Closes,
A Window Usually Opens In Its Place

Printed December 2013

So I'm lying in bed with Dave the other night, watching *Sons of Anarchy* and drifting off to that happy place I go when no one's asking me for money or to drive them somewhere, when my sixteen-year-old comes in to say good night. She tosses her dirty clothes into the hamper (small victory there), spends a few minutes on the floor snuggling with the dog, and then heads for the door.

Innocuous, right? Just another ordinary night.

Maybe in your eyes but not in mine.

For me, the difference between this night and every other night was the absence of one simple, little thing. A thing that I've come to depend on as a mom for the last sixteen odd years. A thing I cherish. The Kiss.

See, I was born the child of snugglers. I was raised as a hugger and a kisser. My people emote. It's just what we do. And so that's how my kids have been raised.

I'm not saying that we kiss each other good-bye when we move from room to room in the house. I mean we're not freaks. But you get the idea. We're all affectionate by nature. And I guess I just always hoped that the strength of my genetics would win out and my kids would bypass the phase where they didn't crave me kissing on them all the time. It was a pipe dream. I know that now.

But as usual, my big mouth grew a mind of its own and decided to call Riley out on why she wasn't kissing me good-night. "What? You can't kiss your mother good-night anymore?" were the words I think I used. I know, very Seinfeld. And a huge tactical error. I can see that now, because when I write about the asinine things I do, it helps me to view them through a clearer lens and see myself as the idiot that I really am.

It was a big mistake. Huge. It was at the exact moment when my words floated into her ear canal that she froze, turned, and looked at me with that look that said, "Really? Seriously?" Then she kept twisting the doorknob and left the room.

Now any normal person capable of reading the obvious signs would've just cut their losses and backpedaled away from the edge of the cliff. But not me. I'm not known for my smarts, so I just kept on pedaling, yelling something sarcastic through the door.

She never came back. And I guess I can't blame her. I'm also pretty sure I know why she didn't come back—she was taking pity on me, not wanting to admit to me with actual words that she needed something different from me now. And I guess it was my responsibility to realize that just because she didn't need to kiss me good-night anymore didn't mean she didn't need me anymore. And that's on me. That's my pill to swallow. Actually, I guess it's every parent's pill to swallow.

But in the heat of that moment, a tectonic plate had shifted for me. In that moment when she opted out of the good-night kiss, I began slipping into a crevice between two distinctly different worlds: one where your kids can't live without you and another where they wipe off your kisses and pretend they don't know you.

Now, she'll be seventeen in June, so I get it. I'm not that oblivious. I know there's a lot of emotional posturing going on at her age, and juniors in high school as a whole aren't exactly busting down their parents' door to give out kisses. So I try my best to set the expectations bar low and take into consideration where she's at in her life. I really do. But sometimes I just can't help myself, and the barbed wire fence that surrounds my impulse control gets a chink in it. And then things I'm thinking, that should stay firmly in the back of my mind, sneak out and get me in trouble.

What can I say, I'm only human.

Usually, though, at pivotal moments like that Dave can save me from myself by talking me off the ledge or just throwing himself on top of me like a soldier saving a buddy in the line of fire. But I think he was already dozing off by the time Riley came in to say good night, so he was asleep at the wheel and couldn't save me from myself. Not this time.

Now look, I know my kids love me. That's never been the issue, and I've never doubted it for a second. I guess I just always had this fantasy that they'd always need my crazy lovin' forever. Although now that I think about it, I suppose it would be a little odd to expect Riley to want me to swing by her dorm room every night when she goes off to college and tuck her in. (See, when I put my thoughts down on paper, the ridiculousness of them becomes clear very quickly.)

But I'd be lying if I said I didn't miss the little girl who used to insist I snuggle in her bed until she fell asleep. Because I do. The same little girl who, when she was five, would slap her hands on either side of my face and lay a big, fat, squishy wet one right on my lips. I think about that little girl all the time, and I miss her dearly. Just like I'm sure my mother misses the little me who used to creep under her covers at night during a thunderstorm and sleep pressed up against her.

Because regardless of how optimistic we all are as parents that *our* kids will be different, they rarely are. They all go through some version of the same thing when it comes to outgrowing things that used to be crutches. They all hit that point when they can finally sleep without the light on or with the door closed or without their woobie. And, sadly for us, they also outgrow the need to snuggle under the covers with Mommy and Daddy on Saturday mornings or climb onto our lap while we're reading the paper.

But thankfully, life has a beautiful, subtle way of balancing the scales for us. Meaning that when one door closes, a window usually opens in its place.

Dave reminds me all the time that everything in life is cyclical. We give up one thing, and something else comes around to take its place and balance the load. Like how now, instead of cuddling together watching Saturday morning cartoons, Riley drives me to Starbucks on days when we both have an hour to spare, and we have coffee together and just talk. Different than snuggling, but no less beautiful.

So I suppose it's just as important that we, as parents, evolve and mature right along with our kids to make the sting of them growing up bite a little less. That and dreaming about being able to cuddle with grandchildren someday helps, too. But I'm OK waiting a little longer for that. She's not even seventeen, for God's sake.

When Life Gives You Lemons,
Squeeze the @#%! Out of Them

Printed December 2013

Adkdalksf wkjgfw swlgfjergjeg eeqkfkewo wkf slkfjwj efrfsdfkjdf! Madjakdw cad d fjswjefw swjfsfjer fakwdw. Sdlfakj jad fkenvia, adj, adjad, adjf, nfpaqf!!

That's not a typo. That's a visual representation of how fast my mind is racing right now. Truth is, I feel like I just ripped into a sleeve of Double Stuf Oreos and let all their crack-like properties swim around my brain.

I'm crazy in the head because my kids flew down to Florida to visit their grandparents for the week.

A! WEEK! I know. We've won the lottery.

So my mind racing is not a product of nerves. It's excitement. Sheer, raw excitement. Like the kind you felt when you turned twenty-one and you walked into your first bar and got served for the first time and it was legit. (Which, Mom, by no means implies that I used a fake ID at any point prior to that.)

Even though this is the first time we've put our kids on a plane by themselves, I'm good. Like really, really good. I mean, they're almost seventeen and fourteen. If this were the 1800s, they'd both have their own kids by now. So that helps me keep a three-hour solo flight to West Palm Beach in perspective. Plus, they've both flown enough in their lives to know the drill in their sleep.

I grilled them both until they were cross-eyed, so they're solid. Cross-body bags will be worn as such; wallets will be stowed at the bottom of their bags; only a moron would forget to apply their sunscreen; strangers will not be spoken to unless they're famous or extremely good looking; luggage will *not* be left unattended; and all seat backs and tray tables will be returned to their upright positions upon descent. These little nuggets of travel truth have been burned into their brains, so in my opinion, they were ready.

How did this little Christmas miracle happen? Well, we can thank my parents and my in-laws. Who, by the way, I've never loved more than I do at this exact moment. God, I love you guys.

More importantly, though, what are Dave and I going to do with this little gift from heaven? Uh, seriously? The question isn't "What *are* we going to do," the question is "What *aren't* we going to do?"

Growing up, we had this cute little sign over the sink in our downstairs bathroom that said, "When life gives you lemons, make lemonade." I never paid much attention to it when I was a kid, to be honest. But the second our parents told us they were sending for the girls for the week, that little sign flashed up in my mind like the ABC SuperSign electronic billboard in Times Square. Needless to say, we're gonna squeeze the living @#$! out of those lemons this week. Gonna drain 'em dry.

So that's why my head is spinning so fast. Because I know we did all kinds of amazing stuff BK (Before Kids), but the problem is, it's all rushing back into my head all at once, so my brain looks kind of like the inside of Filene's Basement when they had their annual bridal gown sale. Utter chaos.

Realistically, I think I'll probably need the first day or two just to decompress and readjust. I mean you can't just shift gears from June Cleaver to Kim Kardashian overnight. That kind of an adjustment takes at least twenty-four to thirty-six hours. Then, once we're in the eating-dinner-at-eleven-thirty groove again, we can really hit the ground running.

First order of business: Crank up a little *Old Time Rock and Roll*, throw on some tighty-whities, and slide the dining room floor, Joel

Goodsen style. And don't pretend you wouldn't do it if your kids were gone, too. You know you would.

Being temporarily kidless kind of has that kid-in-a-candy-store quality. So much to do, so little time. I feel compelled to do stuff I haven't done in ages, but the problem is I'm just not sure I'm that girl anymore, now that I'm right in the thick of it.

I mean, I know we should probably find out what the hot clubs are and go there. Or have a kegger. Or borrow somebody's Porsche and do donuts in the temple parking lot. But honestly, I'm kinda tired and I've been trying to finish the same book since July and this might be my only shot.

I know there have been literally thousands of amazing things I've wanted to do that have crossed my mind when I'm waiting in the pickup line at the high school or standing in line at Crosby's, but now that the decks are clear and we've got carte blanche, I just don't think I'm up for it. And neither, frankly, is Dave.

We're losers. And we know it. But between you and me, we both like it that way.

Yeah, we'll probably go out to eat around eight thirty one night, if we can make it that late, just to prove to ourselves that we've still got game. And maybe we'll grab dinner in the North End one night, just to make sure we get off the peninsula at least once. (Although we'll probably end up calling Donna at Café Italia and reserving a high top because we're too lazy to drive into the city.) Other than that, we're both secretly thrilled to run ourselves down to the Driftwood every morning for brunch and then plant ourselves at Starbucks for a few hours to catch up on reading. (Don't tell my editor, Kris, but I'm almost always at least three weeks behind reading my *Reporter*. Sad irony there, I know.)

Beyond that, the reality of our big week alone will probably look a lot like this: sleep in until the dog wakes us up at six forty-five, text the girls, go for a run, do some lighter-than-usual laundry, text the girls again, talk about dinner, run a few errands, call the girls, read a little, talk more about dinner, go crazy and watch some *Boardwalk Empire* in the afternoon, a little yoga, straighten up the girls' rooms (sorry girls, I can't let this golden opportunity go), take a walk, eat dinner, drink some wine, watch a few extra episodes of *The Big Bang Theory*, call the girls to say good night, and read another few pages before we fall asleep with our glasses on. Anything else is none of your damn business.

The irony is it will be absolutely perfect, in spite of how lame it seems from the outside. Perfect for us anyway. Because as we move from stage to stage along this little journey we all take, our needs change in striking ways. We settle into these perfect little grooves of our life that are sometimes so different than the grooves we started in. But somehow they become the exact place we really want to be. It's beautiful, really, how it all happens kind of organically.

So yes, of course I'm thrilled beyond words with the freedom and quiet we'll have this week, but I'm sure I won't make it to Wednesday before I'll be ready for my kids to come home. Because the fact is, as much as there are times when I'd give anything to be alone with Dave on some tropical island in some little shack on stilts, at the end of the day, I love the craziness of my little life too much to want to be away from it for too long. And I'll bet you'd be feeling the same way if you were in my shoes.

Rest assured, I'll definitely be making plenty of lemonade this week, but I'll be making it exactly the way I like it, simple and sweet.

Afterword

I couldn't properly end this book without a quick word about the unconventional way it came to be.

You already know that it was inspired by my family, my friends, and my hometown. But what you don't know is how this project made it from my laptop to the slick little book you're holding in your hands.

Now I could've gone the more traditional publishing route and tried to shop my book around to publishers to see if anyone would bite. And the best-case-scenario reality of that decision would've meant waiting three to four years to publish my book. But considering that I've dreamed of publishing a book since I was six, I wasn't too keen on waiting another four years. I'm just too damn impatient for that. So I opted to self-publish, the beauty of which is that I get to maintain 100 percent of the creative control over my project and it's way quicker.

The only downside to self-publishing is that the cost of producing your own book falls directly on you. And with my oldest daughter only a year away from going off to college, I couldn't, in good conscience, take anything away from her college fund to make this project happen. Can't you just see it: "Sorry, honey. No college this year, Mommy's gonna try to publish her book instead." Call me crazy, but it just didn't seem fair.

Enter my brilliant husband, Dave, who told me about this amazing Internet crowd-funding platform called Kickstarter that helps bring creative projects to life.

It's a simple concept, really. You create a campaign to promote your project—whatever creative project that happens to be—and you launch it on the Kickstarter website. Then, if people like what they see, they pledge whatever amount they want to support you. And if you hit 100 percent of whatever your funding goal is before your campaign deadline ends, your project becomes a reality.

Since its launch in 2009, the New York-based web portal has helped more than five million people successfully fund their creative projects—everything from music and technology to film and publishing.

So that's what I did. I developed a pitch to market my book, launched a thirty-day Kickstarter campaign, and then blasted it out to the world on Facebook (www.facebook.com/ItIsWhatItIsColumn) and other social media. And within the first two weeks of the campaign, I reached my funding goal. It was incredible, really. I had pledges in all denominations pouring in from everywhere—from people I knew and from people I didn't. It was truly amazing and humbling all at the same time. It's like Dave says, this is what the Internet economy is all about: enabling people, like me, without contacts or funding to successfully bring a project to life. And the best part of it for me is that the people who read and love my work are the ones who enabled this project to become a reality.

Life: It Is What It Is truly is a book for the people by the people. And I can honestly say, all said and done, that the journey of writing this book has been one of the greatest of my life—living proof that life is always a work in progress and you just have to keep moving forward toward whatever goals you have.

So now that you know how my book came to be, here's a list of the people who made it happen. To all of you, thank you, thank you, *thank you* for paying it forward and believing in me. I couldn't have done it without you.

Thank you, Natalie Belli; thank you, Doreen Bentley; thank you, EuRim Chun; thank you, Patti Chrzan; thank you, Jenni and Chris Clock; thank you, Karen and Tim Conley; thank you, Melissa Crane; thank you, Stephanie and Scott Curran; thank you, Amy and Bill

Cunningham; thank you, Theresa McGuinness-Darby and Dave Darby; thank you, Blakeslee and Brett Detels; thank you, Kathy and Jim Doody; thank you, Julie and John Duggan; thank you, Dineen Ehrenberg; thank you, Sandy Eigner; thank you, Ronnie Feldman; thank you, Jenny and David Frontero; thank you, Whitney and Mike Gillett; thank you, Amy and Pat Gilligan; thank you, Doreen Godes; thank you, Erin and Al Hart; thank you, Dianne and Steve Hatfield; thank you, Beezee and Tom Honan; thank you, Kim and Mike Kramer; thank you, Drew, Geoff, Emily, and Alden Lemieux; thank you, Charlotte Mazonson; thank you, Paul and Kathie Mazonson; thank you, Lisa McCarthy; thank you, Ilana and Greg Mogolesko; thank you, Ben and Michelle Motolla; thank you, Mandy and Craig Murphy; thank you, Lisa and David Nagel; thank you, Tammy and Dick Nohelty; thank you, Kristen, Jim, and Chloe Noonan; thank you, Tracy and Marc Orloff; thank you, Annie Pugh; thank you, Kara and Ian Pugh; thank you, Scott and Gaynor Rabin; thank you, Michael and Tricia Rockett; thank you, Pam Rockett Castner; thank you, Lauren, David, Peter, and Kate Santeusanio; thank you, Kara and Tony Scivetti; thank you, Lora and Marvin Steinberg; thank you, David, Riley, and Libby Sugarman; thank you, Stan and Evelyne Sugarman; thank you, Jennifer and Corey Tapper; thank you, Meredith and Jamie Tedford; thank you, Amy and Guy Tully; thank you, Sara Thatcher and Greg Dombal; thank you, Frank White; thank you, Gail Woodrow; thank you, Shelly and Alan Zelbow. And thank you to everyone who believed in me and in this book. I'm truly grateful.

Special Thanks

And special, special thanks to Natalie Belli, Nikki Sabin, and Hilary Van Dusen for giving me guidance and direction that made all the difference in the world.

About LISA SUGARMAN

I've been a writer most of my life, so this book has been cooking for a really, really long time. I actually can't remember a time when I didn't have a pencil in my hand or a cheap spiral notebook in my bag. In fact, one of my earliest memories goes back to age six or seven when I started a neighborhood newspaper with my friend Stacey. We were a one-hit wonder, though. We released one issue and then hung it up. Probably to play Barbies. But I still have that newspaper, and I still love to write, more than just about anything. And I've been doing it one way or another for almost the last forty years— writing for everything from newspapers and magazines to marketing and publishing companies. But I really found my sweet spot with my opinion column, "It Is What It Is," published by GateHouse Media, Inc. I've been writing "It Is What It Is" for the *Marblehead Reporter* since 2009, and that's how this book was born.

My style is simple. I'm direct. I'm opinionated. I'm emotional. I'm fair. And some say I'm funny. (I like them.) I've got an incredibly long stream of consciousness with endless opinions on everything from life and parenting to relationships and health and everything in between.

But the truth is, I'm a very simple wannabe farm girl who loves to write and loves to tell it like it is.

I'm also a wife. A mom. A columnist. And I guess now, an author. But I'm also umpteen other things. So you'll just have to do a little reading to find out what else. I hope you enjoy reading it half as much as I enjoyed writing it.

Made in the USA
Charleston, SC
19 June 2014